Business Perspective Investing

And Why Financial Numbers Are Not Important When Picking Shares

By **Roger W. Lawson**

Published by:
Roliscon Ltd
PO Box 62
Chislehurst, Kent
BR7 5YB, UK

Tel: +44-20-8295-0378
Web: www.roliscon.com

First published in the United Kingdom 2019
Printed in the United Kingdom by CPI Group, Croydon
Copyright © Roliscon Ltd 2019
Roliscon is a trademark of Roliscon Ltd

ISBN: 978-0-9545396-3-4

Contents

About the Author 8

Who Should Read This Book and Dedication 9

Preface 10

1. Why Accounts Don't Matter 11
- Accrual Accounting Can Mislead 12
- Accounts Don't Tell You About the Future 12
- Accounts Mainly Tell You About the Past 14
- Management Competent and Trustworthy? 15
- Examples of How Accounts May Mislead 16
- Better Measures of the Quality of a Business 17
- SWOT Analysis 18
- Quality is the Key 19

2. Business Models & Competitive Strategy 19
- Generic Strategies 19
- Barriers to Entry 20
- Differentiated Products 22
- Small Transactions or Large? 22
- Long Term Contracts 23
- Diverse Clients and Suppliers 23
- Capital Requirements 24
- Vertical Integration 24
- Network Effects and Natural Monopolies 25
- Regulations Can Create Barriers to Entry 26
- Do You Understand the Business Model? 26
- Do You Understand the Competitive Threats? 27
- Is a Company in a Sector You Like? 28
- Investor Checklist 34

3. Market Position, Branding & Marketing 35

- One Product or Many? 35
- Branded Products or Commodities? 36
- Trade Mark Registration and Internet Use 37
- Leading Brand Positions 37
- Brand Valuations 38
- Product in Harmony with Economic Trends 39
- Does a Product Add Value? 39
- Product Competently Marketed 39
- Investor Checklist 40

4. Controlling Risk 41

- What Risks is a Company Facing? 41
- The Risk of New Competitors 42
- The Risk of Technological Obsolesence 43
- The Risk of Market Changes 43
- The Risk of Government Regulation 43
- The Risk of Failure to Develop a New Product 44
- Production Process Risk 44
- Risk of Reputation and Brand Damage 45
- The Risk of Management Incompetence 45
- The Risk of Fraud and False Accounting 46
- Debt Risk 47
- Exchange Rate Risk 48
- Business Acquisition Risk 48
- Foreign Adventures Risk 49
- Controlling Risk & Paranoid Management 51
- Investor Checklist 52

5. Rational Pricing and Good Margins 53

- Creating and Maintaining Good Margins 54
- Investor Checklist 54

6. Company Culture, Structure & Pay 55

- ➤ An Appropriate Culture 55
- ➤ Founders and Succession 56
- ➤ Executive Chairmen 58
- ➤ Company Structure 59
- ➤ Motivated and Happy Staff 59
- ➤ Environmental, Social and Governance (ESG) 60
- ➤ Ethically Sound? 61
- ➤ Remuneration 62
- ➤ Flash Offices and Excessive Perks 64
- ➤ Investor Checklist 64

7. Company Regulation And Governance 65

- ➤ Company Domicile 65
- ➤ Applicable Listing Rules 66
- ➤ Corporate Governance Code 66
- ➤ Large or Small Director Share Stakes 69
- ➤ Director Share Sales and Purchases 70
- ➤ Too Many Directors 70
- ➤ Too Many Jobs 70
- ➤ AGMs – When, Where and Well Run? 71
- ➤ Prejudicial Share Placings 71
- ➤ Share Buy-Backs 72
- ➤ Share Liquidity and Bid/Offer Spreads 73
- ➤ Speculative Interest & Too Much Discussion 73
- ➤ Legal Disputes? 74
- ➤ Large Pension Liabilities? 74
- ➤ Have You Read the Annual Report? 74
- ➤ Directors Acting in Your Interests or Theirs? 74
- ➤ Investor Checklist 76

8. Presentation of Accounts 77
➢ EBITDA or Not? 77
➢ Exceptional Items and Adjusted Profits 78
➢ Examples of Adjustments – 80
➢ Adjustments Made in the Accounts of Banks 81
➢ Confusing Accounts Confuse Investors 82
➢ Prudent, Understandable and Consistent 82
➢ Presentation Dissonance 83
➢ Directors Comments 83
➢ Conclusion 83
➢ Investor Checklist 84

9. Systems and Operations 85
➢ Some of the Worst Failings 85
➢ Judging the Quality of Systems & Operations 86
➢ Gradual Improvement or Revolution 87
➢ Summary – Change is Good 89
➢ Investor Checklist 90

10. Financial Analysis 91
➢ Problems with P/E Ratios 91
➢ Growth Needs to be Taken into Account 92
➢ Styles Go In and Out of Favour 92
➢ Adding More Factors 93
➢ Avoiding Disasters 93
➢ Stock Screens 94
➢ Some Ratios Don't Work for Some Stocks 95
➢ Can You Trust Analysts' Forecasts? 96
➢ Financial Analysis and Styles 96
➢ What the Author Considers 98
➢ Assets That are Difficult to Value 105
➢ Trends More Important 105
➢ Investor Checklist 106

11. Trusts and Funds 107
- ➤ Consistent Long-Term Performance 108
- ➤ Active Versus Passive 108
- ➤ Experienced Fund Manager With a Process? 108
- ➤ Not a Closet Index Tracker 109
- ➤ Low Cost 109
- ➤ Not Too Large 109
- ➤ Board Engaged and Independent 109
- ➤ Performance Fees 110
- ➤ Controlled Discount 110
- ➤ Reasonable Discount 111
- ➤ Look At Underlying Holdings & Performance 111
- ➤ AGMs Well Run 111
- ➤ Informative Annual Reports 112
- ➤ Investor Checklist 112

12. Key Lessons & Conclusions 113
- ➤ Research, Research, Research 113
- ➤ Learn From Your Mistakes 114
- ➤ Conclusion 115
- ➤ Investor Checklist 116

Investor Checklist Summary 117

About the Author

Roger Lawson obtained a first degree in production engineering and a Masters Degree in Business Administration from Cranfield Business School. He started his working career as a programmer on IBM mainframe systems, moving on to consulting in software houses followed by some years as the IT Director of a major retailer in the UK.

He then set up a software company called Proactive Systems (before "proactive" became an overused word) which sold system utility products to mid-range users—mainly database tools, report writers and latterly electronic form products. After two rounds of venture capital investment and growing to an international operation with offices in the USA, France and Germany plus a network of distributors, the business was sold in a trade sale to Nasdaq quoted JetForm (subsequently Accelio).

Thereafter he set up and worked as Managing Director of Stream-Serve UK, a business focused on output management, information delivery and e-business communication with a Swedish parent company, and also made a number of "business angel" investments in start-up and early stage businesses as well as acted as a non-executive director in such businesses. He currently runs his own management consulting firm and manages a large portfolio of quoted companies. He has been a director of both ShareSoc and UKSA, two organisations which represent the interests of private shareholders and has a particular interest in shareholder rights, investor education and stock market regulation on which he has written extensively.

His previous books include "Beware the Zombies: How to Manage a High-Tech Business" - A book of practical ideas for solving day to day business problems in high technology companies.

Roger Lawson publishes a blog on financial matters here: https://roliscon.blog and can be followed on Twitter: @RogerWLawson

Who Should Read This Book

This book is aimed at stock market investors who invest directly in listed companies, whether you are a private investor or institutional fund manager. It will help you to analyze companies and pick out those that are good long-term investments. It may not help you if you are a short-term speculator or someone who aims to get rich quickly. As many private investors invest in a mix of direct shares and investment trusts or funds, there is also a chapter on the latter.

This book provides a different approach to the selection of good investments rather than the typical emphasis on financial numbers.

For the mathematically incompetent, this book will create no fears. By taking a different approach to most investment books, it might enable you to identify companies that are sound investments before the financial numbers demonstrate that fact, and perhaps more importantly, enable you to avoid the investment dogs of this world that are at risk from lurking and unsuspected problems in their businesses.

Dedication

This book is dedicated to all those who I learned from during my business and investment career on what makes a good company. And to my long-suffering wife Christine - it's never easy being married to a workaholic.

Preface

Investing in individual stock market shares is not a simple task. You need to learn many skills to be a successful investor – which I define as someone who can achieve better investment returns than the average of the market over an extended period of time, or at least in the sectors in which you choose to invest.

There are many skills you need to learn to be successful. For example, you need to learn how to manage risk, how to trade so as to back your winning share picks and cut those that are doing badly, and how to analyze company accounts.

Where do you start when building a portfolio? Many people begin by picking shares in companies that look the most attractive financially. They use stock screens to find the most profitable, those that are cheapest based on a price/earnings ratio or return on capital, those that pay the best dividends, or otherwise come out well on one or more financial ratios. You can buy books that tell you which ratios, or combination of ratios, are those most correlated with future share price performance.

But this book argues that financial ratios are not the most important aspects to look at when selecting company shares. Heresy you may say. But I will try and convince you otherwise.

This book explains what you should really be looking at if you are to avoid the dogs of the investment world, and pick the winners instead.

Roger W. Lawson

London, June 2019

Chapter 1

Why Accounts Don't Matter

"The difficulty lies not so much in developing new ideas, but escaping from old ones"........ John Maynard Keynes.

Financial accounts don't matter for several reasons:

1. They cannot be relied upon.
2. They only represent a snapshot of the business at one point in time.
3. They may tell you little about the future.
4. They don't tell you whether the management are competent and trustworthy.

The Annual Report of a company is well worth reading, but even for large FTSE companies where their business strategy should be described, they hide a lot of very important information.

> **Point # 1**
>
> Accounts cannot be relied upon.

The number of cases where investors have discovered that the accounts of a company were misleading, or even a total work of fiction are numerous. For example in the UK: **Connaught, NCC Group, Autonomy, Cedar Group, iSoft, Utilitywise, Quindell, Mitie, Conviviality, Amey, Capita, Carillion, Cattles, Healthcare Locums, Erinaceous, Findel, Northern Rock, HBOS, Royal Bank of Scotland (RBS), Torex Retail, Silverdell, Globo, Patisserie, Polly Peck, Maxwell Communications, Conviviality** and many, many more which are too numerous to mention. That's apart from major US cases such as **Enron** and **Worldcom**. The above examples include both small and large companies and although smaller companies can be perceived as being riskier, in reality even the largest companies can collapse at short notice. Some of the above were FTSE-100 companies.

Not all of these companies were the victims of deliberate fraud. Many were simply examples of management's proclivity to present optimistic figures to investors. Or at least ones that met analysts' forecasts and enabled them to achieve their bonus targets.

Accrual Accounting Can Mislead

Accrual accounting is the basis for IFRS and other accounting standards. It attempts to match future revenue and costs. Future costs may already be incurred, and future revenues already contracted for and billed, but the cash movements may differ very considerably. The cash movements may not reflect the underlying position of the business. Therefore it is widely accepted that accrual accounts provide a more accurate and consistent view.

But accrual accounting requires estimates by management. On revenues it enables recognition of revenues that are not yet invoiced – for example on long term contracts. Whether the future cash flows will match is often a difficult question to answer.

Accounts Don't Tell You About The Future

Why do people invest in the shares of public companies? In essence, and ignoring the speculators, they do so because they expect to receive more in the future by investing now – it's gratification postponed. That means more in terms of capital appreciation and dividends, i.e. total return, in future time periods from their initial investment than originally invested. The value of a business is dependent on future cash flows.

> **Point # 2**
>
> The value of a business depends on future cash flows.

Investors should preferably be doing a discounted cash flow calculation, either directly or implicitly, on the future cash flows from owning the company. That includes the dividends receivable and the likely cash they can realize from selling the shares in the future. Estimating the future values requires estimation of future earnings and future asset valuations of a business. But typical ratios used by investors to evaluate and compare companies tell you almost nothing about the future.

12

The commonest ratio used is the price/earnings ratio (P/E) which tells you how much you are paying for the current profits of a company. This is typically based on the historic profits (one year in the past), or one year in the future based on analysts' estimates for the current year.

But what are the profits? Pre-tax, or post-tax? Earnings before Interest, Taxes, Depreciation and Amortization (EBITDA), or "reported" earnings? Underlying profits or not? See Chapter 8 for a discussion of the confusing complexity that has crept in to accounting statements.

Alternative valuation measures are the dividend yield, which is totally at management's discretion even if it does tell you how much cash you may receive in the short term from an ordinary share investment in the company, or measures of the assets held by the company.

Assets used to be a very good measure of the current and potential future value of a company as they can represent productive earnings capability. For example, machinery installed or property owned. But many companies in the modern era rely for their earnings potential on intangible property that may be inadequately valued by conventional accounting. For example, software IP or brands. Or the earnings may be a reflection of the employees' revenue generating capability through the provision of services, or the contracts the company has with third parties. For that reason assets tend not to be used to value companies in modern times unless they are property companies or are suffering financial distress (e.g. are no longer a "going concern" when people start looking at how much the assets could be sold for in a fire sale).

Assets are valued only at a single point in time, and forecasting their future value is often problematic. Indeed in the case of banks, where loans may be anticipated to likely default in future, IFRS does not permit the prudent recognition of that fact. Only actual losses can be reflected in the accounts. This was one cause of the excessively optimistic view of the financial position of banks prior to the financial crisis in 2008.

Accounts Mainly Tell You About the Past

Financial accounts reflect how good the business model of the company has been in the past in generating profits and cash.

A company's business model describes how the organization creates, delivers, and captures value via its adopted business processes. The accounts are only a good pointer to the future if the world, and the markets in which the company operates, are in stasis, i.e. nothing about the market and the company is going to change. That's a very big assumption in the modern world!

Management Competent and Trustworthy?

One of the key factors that affect the outcome of any investment is the competence of the management and how much they can be trusted to look after your interests rather than their own. That is particularly so when investing in smaller or unlisted companies.

Incompetent or inexperienced management can screw up a good business in no time at all, although the bigger the company, the less likely it is that one person will have an immediate impact. But Fred Goodwin allegedly managed to turn the **Royal Bank of Scotland (RBS)**, at one time the largest bank in the world, into a basket case that required a major Government bail-out in just a few years. It's possible that he might claim there were other causes or contributors to the debacle. But few people would argue that Goodwin's aggressive personality did not affect the outcome. Many shareholders, including former employees of the bank, were impoverished and some made bankrupt due to the share price collapse.

Royal Bank of Scotland remained a bank and many of its operations remained the same, but the strategy adopted of taking on more risk, not just by reducing capital adequacy but my pursuing risky acquisitions, undermined the business and brought its downfall.

The moral is that one cannot assume that what makes a company profitable in the past will continue to do so in the future if management changes strategy or makes poor operational decisions.

Examples of How Accounts May Mislead

Financial accounts and conventional valuation metrics used by many investors are particularly misleading when valuing early stage companies, or those rapidly growing. A conventional p/e ratio ignores the future growth in earnings that on a discounted cash flow basis will add substantial value.

Jim Slater attempted to tackle that issue by inventing the Price Earnings Growth Ratio (PEG) that adjusts for the rate of growth in earnings. But that is a rather simplistic approach and cannot be applied if the company has no current earnings.

For example, **Amazon** apparently took a strategic decision to grow the company some years ago as opposed to maximizing short term profits. As a result it reported losses in 2014 and prior years and was still valued at $150 billion at the 2014 year end! The company has subsequently continued to grow and is reporting profits at the time of writing but is on the sky-high p/e of 95. Needless to point out perhaps that it is not paying a dividend. So investors clearly have taken a view on the future ability of the company's business model to continue to be successful in terms of gaining market share with the prospect of market dominance and future profits.

Or take that other big internet success story, **Facebook**. It was founded in 2003 and grew to 1 billion users by 2012. Initially there seemed to be little attention to how the users could be "monetized" but an advertising model was soon adopted. The year 2012 was the year when it did an IPO, but it still lost $59 million in that year. The IPO valued the company at over $100 billion! That made it the third largest IPO in American history. Like Amazon, investors were obviously forecasting that the company would continue to grow both its users and that profits would subsequently appear, as they have done. Users are now over 2 billion, at the time of writing.

The same can be true of many relatively new smaller companies, and not just technology or internet-based ones. A good example is **Purplebricks**, an on-line estate agency. It currently has a market cap of £500 million but has never made a profit. Losses are actually increasing and the share price has been falling in the last year as doubts are raised about its business model.

But still some investors are clearly willing to invest in it, or continue to hold the shares in anticipation of future profits. Such investors are rather like those who invest in new gold mines on the principle that it might make them as rich as Croesus. It rarely does of course but hope springs eternal. Perhaps Purplebricks is an extreme case, but there are many similar examples.

Investors hope that on-line estate agents will mainly replace traditional ones with new low-cost operating structures and lower customer fees, and that Purplebricks will become the dominant player or "gorilla" in its marketplace. I would not like to predict whether that will be the case or not but clearly there are competitors in that space and low barriers to entry so they are in a market share "land grab" as it is called so as to establish a dominant position while it is still possible to do so.

An alternative shorthand approach to valuing such companies as opposed to doing a full ; analysis is to use a revenue multiple (market cap divided by historic or future revenue). On that basis Purplebricks is valued at 5.5 times last year's revenue. If it was not making big losses, the multiple would likely be higher.

You could of course do a full cash flow analysis based on forecasting future revenues and operating costs, but such forecasts can be wildly inaccurate more than a year or two hence. And what discount rate do you apply anyway?

Now you might say that valuing unprofitable companies is a mug's game and that you will never invest in such companies. But by doing so you are likely to miss out on substantial portfolio returns. The key point being made here is that the market has no problem with valuing such companies.

A share price of any company, whether it is listed or unlisted, is determined by what a willing buyer is willing to pay a willing seller, and in every stock market trade, for every buyer there is a seller.

John Maynard Keynes pointed out that stock markets are more like a beauty parade than a rational valuation process. To quote: "It is not a case of choosing those [faces] that, to the best of one's judgment, are really the prettiest, nor even those that average opinion genuinely thinks the prettiest. We have reached the third degree where we devote our intelligences to anticipating what average opinion expects the average opinion to be."

> **Point # 3**
>
> The stock market is a beauty parade.

Better Measures of the Quality of a Business

If you look at the financial accounts of a company alone, then you are missing out on those aspects of the business that show you how it generates profits and cash. Such measures can tell you more about the likely future success of the business and the risks that it will face. In other words, alternative measures tell you much more about the "quality" of a business and its attractiveness to investors, which are important in the beauty parade of the stock market.

The "quality" of the business, and the capabilities of the management, are the biggest influence on the future profits and return on capital of a company. Actually determining the quality of a business and its earning potential is not easy. But there are many pointers that can help you decide.

Another factor that needs to be taken into account is how risky is the business, i.e. how volatile the future profits might be, and whether they face risks that might fatality undermine the company. It is the "risk adjusted returns" that matter to investors. There are some fairly simple things you can look at to see whether a business is risky or not.

SWOT Analysis

One useful technique to use when looking at a business is a SWOT analysis where SWOT stands for strengths, weaknesses, opportunities and threats. This is a technique invented in the 1960s which became a favourite of MBAs and management consultants. It is a good way to identify and highlight in a one-page quadrangle the key strategic and operational issues that a company faces. It can be a useful approach to identifying some of the non-financial aspects of a company that are worth looking at. Many of the aspects to be examined will be covered in later chapters of this book.

Quality is the Key

This book will attempt to cover what investors should look at when valuing companies, in additional to conventional financial metrics. The key to successful investment is to identify those aspects of a company that make it a high quality business and which will enable it to generate a superior return on capital in the long term.

There are thousands of listed companies you can invest in, so why bother with those that are low quality or high risk? Let the speculators and those with short term horizons waste their money on bad investment choices.

Note: There is a checklist at the end of each chapter after this one, and a summary at the end of the book, so that you can easily rate prospective investments on the perspective of quality.

Chapter 2

Business Models & Competitive Strategy

I want a business with a moat around it and with a very valuable castle in the middle"....... Warren Buffett.

Business models explain how a company uses its operations to generate profits and cash. Models can vary from industry to industry but even within the same industry, business models can vary substantially. For example, those selling equipment can choose to sell their products outright or choose to rent their products to customers. Some companies may be vertically integrated whereas others might choose to outsource their production requirements. Some companies may choose to own their capital assets (such as equipment or buildings) while others may simply lease or rent them.

How companies choose to operate can determine their relative profitability. But even when profitability is similar, some models are better than others in the perception of investors. Investors value certainty so a more stable revenue and profitability model is preferred. A bank or a property company that takes more risks will undoubtedly find its equity shares priced at a lower level than more conservative companies. Future earnings will be discounted to a higher degree due to the relative risk attached to them.

Generic Strategies

Michael Porter in his classic business book entitled "Competitive Strategy" identified three common generic strategies followed by companies: 1) Overall cost leadership; 2) Differentiation and 3) Focus. Cost leadership leads companies to focus on cost control with high capital investment while Differentiation requires strong marketing capabilities, high R&D and organizational strengths.

Focus is a combination of the other policies but directed at a particular target, e.g. market segment. It is important for companies to have a clear, publicly declared strategy along one of those lines. Porter said that the "firm stuck in the middle is almost guaranteed low profitability".

That is because a firm in the middle may lose the high-volume customers who demand low prices, while also missing out on the high-margin business.

It is important for a company's management, and for investors, to understand where the business stands in the competitive environment and how it is going to achieve a superior return on capital (which ultimately drives profits). Superior returns on capital only arise from barriers to entry, or "moats" as famous investor Warren Buffett calls them.

Barriers to Entry

Barriers to entry can arise from the following main sources:

1) Economies of Scale.
2) Product differentiation.
3) Capital Requirements.
4) Switching costs.
5) Access to Distribution Channels.
6) Proprietary technology or Intellectual Property.
7) Access to limited resources (e.g. the best ore deposit).
8) Preferable Government subsidies or regulations.
9) Learning advantage from many years' experience.
10) Network effects.

It is important when looking to invest in a business how easy it will be for competitors to enter their market. Will it be low cost to do so, can they copy the product/service easily, can they poach staff or hire them easily, can they take over the distribution channels easily? Those are some of the key questions.

Let's take some examples:

The volume car market is dominated by a few major international players – General Motors, Ford, Toyota, Fiat/Chrysler, VW, Toyota, Nissan, Hyundai and Honda with a few other European makers following behind such as BMW, PSA, Daimler and Renault. The fact that there are so many tells you that competition is quite fierce and that there is relatively little product differentiation – what competition there is tends to be on price. As a result car manufacturers have had a patchy record of profitability in recent years (GM went bankrupt in 2009).

As major capital items for the average purchaser, these companies also suffer when the general economy in a country is poor and the market also tends to be cyclical as vehicle life can be easily extended by just "putting off" the replacement. But still new entrants are not deterred. For example **Tesla** spent $1.4 billion on R&D in 2017 alone developing the Model 3 and other products. They are trying to enter the volume car market. Although they only have a very limited product range and a poor distribution network in comparison with more established manufacturers, they are betting on superior technology and a focus on one segment (electric cars). Their expenditure on R&D is still a small fraction of what the larger manufacturers spend every year. Apart from the enormous funding requirement they lack the experience of established car manufacturers. Tesla as a company is a bet that many investors would avoid simply because of the risks associated. It seems there are barriers to entry in the car manufacturing market, but clearly not enough to deter new entrants. Large, dominant incumbents and high capital investment required does not necessarily deter new entrants into a market.

Why is **Microsoft** so dominant in PC operating systems? Because after it established an initial dominant position via a tie up with IBM and aggressive marketing, it ensured that the switching costs from other PC operating systems would be very high. Indeed sometimes impossible because the only real alternatives are Apple, or possibly Linux, and third party software products you use may not be available on those platforms. That is why Microsoft continues to have a dominant position in PC operating systems – the barriers to entry are simply too high. The cost of developing an alternative would also be very high – there are reported to be 50 million lines of code in Windows 10.

Barriers to entry are easy to build when you have proprietary products supported by intellectual property that is subject to patents or copyright laws. But car manufacturers are hampered because their products have to conform to regulated standards which means they have tended to become similar.

> **Point # 4**
>
> IP enables barriers to entry.

That is why software companies are often valuable and produce superior returns on capital over the long term, unlike car manufacturers. Microsoft has maintained a high return even though many aspects of its business are relatively mature – the current return on equity is 21%.

Differentiated Products

It is a truism that if multiple companies are selling very similar products, they tend to end up competing on price for new business. Prices tend to regress to the lowest common denominator where at least some suppliers remain. There is very unlikely to be a superior return on capital, and excess profits over the norm, in such companies.

Product or service differentiation enables you to segment markets and undermine competitors – or enter new markets where there is established competition. Software companies can be very attractive for this reason alone – they can often add features to substantially differentiate their product and at relatively little cost, while hardware manufacturers will take much more time to do so.

> **Point # 5**
>
> Product differentiation enables market segmentation.

Small Transactions or Large?

Lumpy revenues, and profits, that arise in companies when they are only making a few sales per year are a negative sign. There is always uncertainty that a sale will be closed so profits can swing wildly from one period to another.

Small, repeat transactions are better. Many retailers have that model, while construction companies are at the opposite end of the spectrum. The latter also suffer from the risk that major projects may overrun or meet technical difficulties. For that reason, construction companies are often lowly rated in the stock market.

Long Term Contracts

Construction companies also suffer from often having long-term contracts that are one-off in nature. Long-term contracts are good only if they mean repeat business on a short-term basis. A typical example is where a product or service is "rented" rather than purchased outright. Software companies have been moving from a one-off license fee to an "SAAS" (software as a service) model because it helps to smooth their cash flow. It's a big advantage when your sales staff don't have to make their targets every month from new business! The desire to hit forecasts of sales and profits when the actual figures are clearly going to fall short is one of the commonest causes of fraudulent financial accounts. The dynamics in such businesses, and how easy they are to manage, are revolutionized by moving to an SAAS model.

> **Point # 6**
>
> Repeat business is what is needed.

Although moving from up-front license fees to an SAAS model does have an impact short-term on cash flow, that is only a one-off change that most businesses can accommodate.

Diverse Clients and Suppliers

A large number of small or diverse customers is a lot better than a few large ones. If a business only has a few customers, sales can be volatile and the customers can hold out for a better deal by sitting on their hands.

> **Point # 7**
>
> Diversity among customers and suppliers is positive.

Likewise having diverse suppliers rather than a few is preferable – the latter can dominate a business unless contracts are well written and watertight, but they will always have pricing power.

23

Capital Requirements

The ideal business is one with low capital requirements. Only such businesses can achieve a high return on capital easily. Those businesses that continually require more capital to match competitive responses, e.g. to invest in more equipment so as to lower production costs, are ones to avoid. Warren Buffett learned this early on when he bought **Berkshire Hathaway** which later formed the core of his investment empire. But when he bought it the company was a textile manufacturer in the USA. To compete with foreign low-cost producers, it needed to invest in ever more expensive manufacturing equipment.

Buffett has claimed that buying Berkshire Hathaway was the biggest investment mistake he ever made and the textile operations were subsequently closed down.

Steel companies also require large amounts of capital – blast furnaces are expensive to both build and maintain. When steel prices are low, steel manufacturers often choose to build new, more efficient plant so that they can achieve lower production costs. As a competitive response, that can be a disaster for investors as other companies follow the same path. The iron/steel sector has traditionally been one to avoid as profits are volatile partly due to the commodity nature of the product and endemic over-capacity.

> **Point # 8**
>
> Low capital required is the best.

Vertical Integration

Some companies are vertically integrated while others are not. For example **Ford** in its early years produced the steel and other primary products that then went into its own cars. This gave it control over the sources of supply and also control over quality. Likewise **Boots the Chemists** used to manufacture many of the drugs that it sold in its retail outlets and could as a result offer very competitive prices.

Other companies choose to outsource manufacturing and simply do the design work – **Apple** is a good example of this model. The modern trend is to outsource more as it provides more flexibility and minimizes capital requirements. **Fevertree** is an example of a company that has currently achieved a great return on capital of 41% because it has contracted out all its bottling. Why own bottling plants when there are a number of suppliers willing to compete for that work? When you are selling a higher margin product it may not matter that your costs will be slightly higher than if you owned your own bottling plant.

It's useful to understand how reliant a company is on third-party suppliers and whether that is a competitive threat or advantage. The threat is that such suppliers could launch their own equivalent products or start to deal with a company's competitors. It may be a short term advantage, but tends to be a long-term disadvantage.

Network Effects and Natural Monopolies

Network effects can give companies a major advantage if they are the "first mover" in a new market. For example, **Facebook** had several competitors in its early years but its member numbers grew to be much larger than others. That means there is a high probability that if you are a Facebook user, then your friends will also be ones. Those that are not will be getting more invites to become Facebook users because more of their friends are using that platform than others. Once dominance is obtained as a result of the network effect, it is very difficult to lose.

> **Point # 9**
>
> Network effects create monopolies.

Some businesses operate in sectors where natural monopolies occur. For example stock markets tend to become monopolies as business gravitates to those markets with the most liquidity, i.e. the bigger markets have an advantage and will tend to grow to become even larger. The retail distribution of electricity and gas is also a natural monopoly as once a supplier has dug up your street to lay the required cables/pipes, a later entrant may get little business. Such companies therefore tend to be heavily regulated by Governments.

Benefiting from network effects and natural monopolies enables companies to achieve a superior return on capital as they create barriers to entry. But Governments often end up regulating such businesses and enforcing a reduction in capital returns.

Regulations Can Create Barriers to Entry

Governments can of course create absolute monopolies by granting rights to do business in particular sectors or geographies. Such monopolies are now relatively rare. But complex and onerous regulations can create barriers to entry and protect incumbents. When the cost of getting regulatory approval is high, and the time to do so is high, it deters new entrants to the market. Much financial regulation is of this nature – it's not easy to open a new bank in the UK for example. You might say that is a good thing to deter dubious new proprietors, but it also plays into the hands of existing banks and reinforces their position.

> **Point # 10**
>
> Regulations can deter new competitors.

Do You Understand the Business Model?

It is important to have a clear understanding of a company's business model before investing in it. It's often obvious – for example a retailing company typically buys in products from third parties and sells them outright to people who either walk in the door or visit their web site. It's that simple. But with other companies it may not be at all obvious.

For example, where there is a mix of services and product sales, it is important to understand the relative proportion and which is the prime focus. The culture and sales/marketing operations tend to be very different in those with a product focus versus those with a services focus.

Is the business model actually simple enough for you to understand it? With early stage technology companies, this can be a problem. They can move from selling directly to selling via distributors, or vice-versa.

26

Newer companies, or those not yet making profits, can change their business models in the hope that a change will improve matters. But it does not always do so.

Do You Understand the Competitive Threats?

It is also important to understand the competitive threats to a company. These can be strategic in nature or tactical, e.g. will general economic or market trends threaten the business, or will specific competitors launch competitive products/services or change their pricing to erode a company's market share?

Companies are often reluctant to talk about the threats from competitors, although it's not difficult to find out who the competitors are by talking to the directors at investor relations events or general meetings.

You can also research trade publications and their web sites, or look at which web sites in the sector are getting the most visitors (there is publicly available data on that for different types of retail products for example). Trade conferences and exhibitions can also be useful sources of information.

For retailers it is easy to walk around their shops and compare them to local competitors, or do the same with their web sites.

For technology companies, there are independent sources of reports on companies focused on a particular subsector, e.g. Gartner reports. Some companies make these available on their web site.

Obviously reading the financial press is a good source of background information on companies and sectors. It is commonplace for successful investors to be avid readers. You can use search engines such as Google to identify any new references to companies in which you are interested, and bulletin boards can help if you can wade through the dross. Sometimes the latter are frequented by employees of the company, and their competitors.

> **Point # 11**
>
> Research the company's market.

In the modern world, your problem will be that there is more information easily accessible than you can possibly digest in a sensible time frame. The key is to delve sufficiently deeply to get some understanding of where a company sits in its market and the stance of major competitors.

You may come across managers of companies that claim the business has no significant competition, e.g. the product or service is unique. This is a warning sign, because it's either bullshit or if true, suggests that there is no developed market for the product/service – that means a lot of market education will be required, which will require up-front capital expenditure. Is there really a demand for the product/service that people are willing to pay for at an economic cost? If there is already an established market then that's usually proof that there is. If there are no competitors, this raises a doubt.

Is a Company in a Sector That You Like?

Experienced investors often have prejudices against particular types of companies. They develop that attitude from experience and the fact that they often do not understand some types of business.

For example, Warren Buffett avoids investing in the tech sector. There may be more than one reason why he avoids such companies. He may simply not understand the business which is one of his key criteria. He prefers businesses that are simple to understand. He has also suggested that it is difficult to pick winners in the technology sector early on and build a position at a reasonable price. But he has invested in some relatively mature technology stocks such as Apple and IBM.

Terry Smith of Fundsmith also has prejudices. Even though he runs a global large cap fund, he has few holdings in banks, insurance or other financial companies, and in mining or oil/gas companies. His main focus is on technology companies (30% at the time of writing), consumer staples (26%) and healthcare companies (26%). He has been one of the most successful UK fund managers in recent years in terms of fund performance.

The author likewise has opinions of which sectors I prefer, and reasons why. Here's a short list, which is not necessarily comprehensive:

a) **Drug development companies.** Reason: so few new drugs actually make it to market. It takes years to get through all the approval stages and the cost can exceed $2 billion. Less than one in ten drugs that enter phase 1 trials actually get to market, and even then a lot of them never recover their costs. But the producers always tell a good story about how their wonder drug will meet a current unmet need and they are helping to cure people of diseases, i.e. it's a major public benefit.

b) **Gold mining companies.** The glitter of gold seems to cause some people to become mentally deranged. The author once invested in an unsuccessful dot.com company which subsequently decided to buy a non-producing goldmine. The directors seemed to be fooled by the seller with prospects of future riches, which needless to say never arrived. Gold and precious metal prospecting companies are definitely to be avoided and even those companies actually producing gold can be exceedingly risky. Apart from operating mainly in countries with political risks all too common, they face regulatory risks and their profitability depends on the price of a commodity. Mark Twain allegedly said all there is to know about gold mine investments: "A mine is a hole in the ground with a liar standing next to it", although the attribution is uncertain as it was a common joke in the mining boom times in the USA.

c) **All mining companies and oil/gas companies.** Just as in gold mining companies, all natural resource companies are very dependent on profitability on the market price of their product over which they have no control at all. They only have control over their costs. Can investors predict the price of a commodity a year or two hence? Which they need to do because developing a new mine or oil field can take years. Any investor who can predict commodity prices is a genius which this writer is not.

Another problem with natural resource companies, as with agricultural product producers, is that they have a natural boom and bust cycle. Prices go up, so producers invest in more production capacity. That takes a year or two to come on-stream and then prices fall due to excess capacity. Excess investment is followed by a financial bust. This cycle is particularly damaging for exploration and early stage developers who may suddenly find that their underground resources are no longer viable to put into production.

d) **Banks.** Before the financial crisis in 2008, major international banks paid high dividends and were generally considered "safe" by conservative investors. Were they not highly regulated, with massive balance sheets and lots of repeat business? But investors ignored the structure of their balance sheets.

This is what the author wrote in a blog article in October 2017 under the headline Why I Still Won't Invest in Banks:

"I do not hold any bank shares at present, and have no plans to change that policy. But I thought it would be worthwhile to look at the results announced by Lloyds Banking Group (LLOY) yesterday for the third quarter. The announced results were positive.

The prospective dividend yield on Lloyds is now near 6% and the p/e is about 9, which is all that some investors look at. The latest balance sheet figures for Lloyds Banking Group show total assets of £810 billion and liabilities of £761 billion, which you might consider safe. But if you look at the asset side there is £161bn in "trading and other financial assets at fair value", i.e. presumably marked to market. They have £27bn in "derivative financial instruments", which Warren Buffett has called "weapons of mass destruction", and £480bn of "loans and receivables", again probably marked to market. Shareholders equity to support the £810bn of assets is £49bn. Which does not strike me as particularly safe bearing in mind what happened in the financial crisis.

For example, that small bank HBOS, which Lloyds bailed out, eventually wrote off £29.6bn alone on their property loans after everyone suddenly realised that their lending had been injudicious and the loans were unlikely to be recovered in full. In addition, banks can conceal their assets and liabilities as we learned at RBS and more recently in the Lloyds case. Indeed tens of billions of loans from Lloyds and others to HBOS were concealed and hidden from shareholders in the prospectus with apparently the consent of the FSA.

So I follow the mantra of Terry Smith of Fundsmith who said in 2013: "We do not own any banks stocks and will never do so having learned from my own experience that it is a very risky, and cyclical sector. I am not convinced that improved regulation, and better capital ratios have made them "investable" when one can invest in other companies with far fewer risks". In his early career Terry Smith was a bank analyst for a City broker.

e) **Insurance and Other Financial Companies.** The whole financial sector can be a tricky one because the accounts of such companies are often difficult to understand and the cash flow statement impenetrable. The assets and liabilities can be misleading – it's no coincidence that the Lloyds of London Insurance Market faced collapse in the 1990s due to unrecognized "long tail" risk on asbestosis claims. If you do not fully understand the accounts of a company, don't invest in it!

f) **Morally dubious businesses.** Companies that operate in the internet gaming sector, in CFD providing, in spread-betting and similar fields are just too subject to regulatory risk. That's apart from the fact that the people running such companies often seem to be untrustworthy and they may be operating from countries which I have developed a prejudice against.

g) **Electronic hardware producers or distributors.** My experience tells me that electronic component manufacturers or distributors are notoriously vulnerable to wide swings in volumes and profits. If they are not selling in cyclical markets, or are vulnerable to stock holding changes, they are vulnerable to rapid product obsolescence and leapfrogging by competitors. This is normally a sector I avoid for those reasons.

h) **Fashion Retailers.** Clothing retailers operating in the fashion sector I avoid because they can go out of fashion, i.e. lose their attractiveness to consumers because they are no longer in tune with the market. Indeed all clothing retailers can be subject to changes in consumer tastes. Consumers can be fickle over what they wear to a much greater extent than for other products or services they buy.

i) **Health Food Product Companies.** Such companies are often peddling what used to be called "snake oil". Unproven remedies for common ailments, or ones that will make you live longer, feel better or even make you perform better in bed.

j) **Construction Companies.** Companies involved in big construction projects are frequently at risk of under-bidding for new business and are then unable to control cost overruns. Sometimes they bid for new business just to obtain some short-term cash flow it seems.

k) **Airlines and Steel Companies.** Both these sectors suffer from the problem of needing to fill capacity and losing money when they do not. An airline has to fly planes on scheduled routes even if there are no passengers and steel producers cannot easily shut down blast furnaces. The temptation is to lower prices to fill capacity but their competitors will do the same, resulting in everyone losing money. It is unclear whether airlines have ever managed to generate a return on the capital invested since most of them were founded in the 1920s.

l) **Recruitment companies and consultancy firms.**
These are very easy to set up and are often very dependent
on the people who run them. There are few barriers to
entry in their markets and the people can walk.

m) **Investment managers.** The profits in such businesses
tend to be taken by the managers, not the shareholders.

I am not saying that some investors cannot make money from
investing in the above sectors. After all there is a price for eve-
rything and the stock market is a way to fix a price that is a
consensus of investors' views. However, the prices of some
types of companies are driven by short-term speculation on
their prospects, often on limited information. No doubt readers will be able to form their own prejudices, given some experience.

Chapter 2 – Investor Checklist

Chapter 2 – Positive Qualities	Tick Here
High barriers to entry?	
Economies of scale?	
Differentiated product/service?	
Low capital required?	
Hard switching costs?	
Proprietary technology and IP?	
Smaller transactions?	
Repeat business?	
Short term contracts?	
Diverse clients?	
Diverse suppliers?	
Network effect benefits?	
Regulations creating barriers to entry?	
Business model simple & understood?	
Competitive threats understood?	
Established market?	
Sector I like?	

Chapter 3

Market Position, Branding & Marketing

"The purpose of business is to create and keep a customer"........
Peter Drucker.

How a company attracts new customers and retains them thereafter is a key aspect to look at when researching companies for investment. Hereafter I will refer solely to products sold but you should read that to include services also – many services are branded in the same way as products which is a very sensible thing for businesses to do.

One Product or Many?

One product companies are exceedingly risky propositions for investors, however good the product. So **Ford** ran into problems when it was only selling the Model T after a few years. Multiple competitors arose who differentiated their products more and sold various "models". Not only that they began to change them every year. That business model in the car industry remains to this day.

If a company only has one product, then it is vulnerable to competitors or any other market or economic circumstances that might change the desirability of its product. Companies can fall into this circumstance unintentionally when one of their products is so successful that it tends to become dominant and others are dropped. At the time of writing, **Apple** is almost in this position with sales of i-Phones more than 50% of revenue while Macs and Watches are far behind. But they do have the i-Tunes ecosystem to fall back on.

One product technology companies are also vulnerable to competitors leapfrogging their technology, and producing new products that erode a company's competitiveness overnight.

> **Point # 12**
>
> Avoid one product companies

You should avoid investing in one product companies. But on the other hand, a company with too many products will lose focus. A multiplicity of undifferentiated brands should be avoided.

Branded Products or Commodities?

Companies that only produce generic commodities should be avoided by investors, or you should at least pay very little for them. Gold miners, miners of all kinds, oil/gas producers and agricultural product producers are of that nature. They cannot differentiate their products to achieve excess profits and the price they can sell the product at will be well outside their control, i.e. they have no "pricing power".

As car manufacturers, soap producers, brewers and gin distillers found out many years ago, the solution is to brand the product with a name (i.e. a trade mark, preferably a registered one). Incidentally the first UK registered trade mark was the **Bass** red triangle used on their IPA beer and registered in 1875. It's still going strong. Trade marks help customers to identify with the product, and make it easier for them to select the product on a new purchase. Brands are particularly effective when there is actually little difference between competitors' products - for example, lager beer, gin or washing powder. Brands are exceedingly valuable if well maintained (which Bass has not always been). **Coca-Cola** is a great example of a powerful brand, supported of course by a "secret recipe".

Popular UK product **Marmite** (a **Unilever** product) is another example of a secret formulation in very recognizable packaging and with a very strong brand name which has been very successful. It has strong customer allegiance and no significant competitors. It would no doubt not have been so successful if it had been labelled "dead yeast" which is basically what it contains, with a few common additives thrown in.

Diageo is a company that focuses on a portfolio of whisky, gin, beer and other alcohol brands and there is little else they talk about. It has consistently achieved a superior return on capital.

Technology companies, particularly early stage ones, can be quite inept in their branding. But just because a product is highly complex does not mean that branding is not a powerful tool. Just consider the names **Rolls-Royce**, **Intel** or **Facebook** for example.

Point # 13 Strong brands are important irrespective of the product.

Producers of technology products and services often ignore the importance of marketing and branding in the mistaken belief that superior technology will always mean that their company will do better than competitors. That is simply not the case.

Strong brands enable higher prices and hence better return on capital, and help to fend off competition and maintain market share.

Trade Mark Registration and Internet Use

It is important that companies which you invest in have protected their brands with registered trade marks and have a strong internet web presence, i.e. have all the similar domain names covered, and they don't have obviously confusing web site names owned by other organisations. This is not often a problem in large companies but it can be in smaller ones.

Leading Brand Positions

Do the company's brands have a market leading position? In other words, are they by revenue the first, second or third brand in the sector being targeted and preferably first or second? Typically companies who are below the third level do not make good profits, if any.

Obviously though different companies can have different market positions in different geographic or other market segments. It is important to understand a company's product positioning in each market segment that it is focused upon.

Point # 14 Need to be in the top 2 of market position.

Brand Valuations

Brands can have a significant impact on a company's valuation. For example, **Diageo** has on its balance sheet £8.9 billion of "brands" under intangible assets.

These assets have sometimes arisen when companies or brands have been acquired and where the company has paid more than the fixed assets acquired. They are annually reviewed for "impairment". Clearly to suggest that brands have no real value is not sensible.

Strong brands, in the sense of high customer recognition and reputation, are exceedingly important to the valuation of any business.

A company's brands can easily be damaged though by corporate mistakes of various kinds. For example, at the time of writing social media companies such as **Facebook** and WhatsApp (owned by Facebook) have reputational problems due to privacy concerns and lack of monitoring of content. The company will probably overcome that short-term impact but others have not with the result that valued brands simply disappear.

Companies can also destroy customer recognition by "rebranding". A classic example of this was the rebranding of **"Royal Mail"** a few years back as **"Consignia"**. Royal Mail was perhaps not a great brand and intrinsically a poor trade mark so there might have been good reasons to invent a new brand. But the change was abandoned after little more than a year and the original name reinstated.

So another question to ask yourself about a company is: Does the company's brand have a good reputation and does the company take active steps to protect that reputation?

> **Point # 15**
>
> Does the company or product have a high reputation?

Product in Harmony with Economic Trends

The population of the world is getting wealthier. Whole countries such as China are developing a new middle-class and even in developed economies the average real income of people is steadily increasing. As people get wealthier, they tend to buy more expensive products so when looking at companies it is important to understand whether they are on the right side of that trend. Companies are also becoming wealthier. Do the products of a company appeal to the poorer consumers and companies or the richer?

Does a Product Add Value?

However, economic value is still important. In economic recessions, consumers and companies become more price sensitive but value is important even in the good times.

One of the key attributes of any new technology product if it is to be a success is whether it adds value. It needs to be not just be a "nice to have" product or based on fashion, but something that contributes to the purchaser's wealth. If it enables a company that purchases the product to produce their own products more cheaply, or faster, or offer services at lower cost, then it will be successful. For industrial products, direct financial advantage is the key. But for consumer products there can be other values that are important. Cosmetics for example add to the beauty of ladies and help them to attract mates, while alcohol and medical products add to wellbeing in different ways.

> **Point # 16**
>
> Does the product add value?

Product Competently Marketed

It is important to emphasize that people and companies buy benefits not features, i.e. they purchase products because of the benefits they endow not because of how they do so. Marketing by a company needs to communicate those benefits clearly and effectively.

A common mistake in all companies is to talk about product features and not benefits. Look at a company's advertising and its web site. Apart from simply promoting brand recognition, does it clearly communicate the benefits?

Chapter 3 - Investor Checklist

Chapter 3 – Positive Qualities	Tick Here
Multiple products/services?	
Strong brands and trade marks?	
Leading market positions?	
In harmony with economic trends?	
Clear value propositions?	
Competent marketing?	

Chapter 4

Controlling Risk

"Only the Paranoid Survive".....title of a book by Andy Grove of Intel.

Investors in companies should be paranoid about the risks that a company is facing in its operations. Modern portfolio theory has suggested that the risk in a share is a function of it's Beta which is a measure of how volatile the share price is relative to the market. This is a very bad measure of the risk of investing in the shares of a company. Volatility in a share price may tell you about the level of speculation, or perceived investor uncertainty about a company, but it tells you nothing about the real threats.

What Risks Is a Company Facing?

For example, in 2010 **BP** was a very large FTSE-100 oil company with a consistent record of paying high dividends. Although profits tended to be somewhat variable as they were dependent on the market price of oil, the company was generally seen as a "safe" share for those with a conservative, low-risk investment focus. In Q4 2009 it paid a dividend of 8.7 pence.

But in 2010 it suffered a major disaster in the Deepwater Horizon oil well explosion and oil spill in the Gulf of Mexico. It killed 15 people and did very widespread environmental damage which certainly had a very negative effect on the reputation of the company. It also meant BP subsequently incurred costs of $62 Billion. The dividend was cancelled for the next three quarters and had still not returned to the 2009 level by 2018. The share price also fell by about 40% in 2010.

Were investors aware of the risks that the company was taking in drilling such deep wells with unproven technology? It would seem not. BP had many other operations and survived the disaster while other companies have been destroyed by such operational mistakes.

Investors need to ask what risks is a company facing. In the Annual Reports of public companies the risks they face are covered and in a Prospectus those risks are covered in even more detail.

The risk faced by investors in a company directly relates to the operational risks associated with the way the company does business and the environment in which it operates. Those risks are affected by many factors and some of them are discussed below.

Point # 17

What are the risks faced by the company?

Most companies run the conventional risks of fire, flood, earthquakes, civil unrest, war and other "natural" disasters but these can usually be insured against. It is also remarkable how rapidly well managed companies can recover from such events. But companies dependent on one location or other resource are ones to be wary of – or ask how they have mitigated that risk by having adequate back-up facilities and procedures.

The Risk of New Competitors

If new competitors enter a market, perhaps attracted by the superior return on capital or excess profits that are obviously being achieved by existing market incumbents, then product margins and profits may be very substantially eroded.

The only way to prevent new competitors entering a market is by having "barriers to entry" as discussed in Chapter 2 of this book. It is important to understand how likely it is that a company will face new competitors. This might be from new low-cost overseas producers (as Warren Buffett suffered from in Berkshire Hathaway when it was manufacturing textiles) or those with a new technological advantage.

Commoditized products are obviously most at risk from price competition whereas strong branding can assist in defending against it.

The Risk of Technological Obsolescence

New technologies can threaten almost all products. Horse buggies and buggy whip manufacturers were mostly put out of business by the invention of the motor car, or they had to adapt to become part of the new industry. But buggy whip producers did not find it easy to do so. From 42 such companies in the nineteenth century in the USA there is perhaps one left (Westfield Whip). The rest went out of business.

> **Point # 18**
>
> Technology and markets can change.

The Risk of Market Changes

Market demand for products and services can change based on new customer demands driven by new perceptions or simply fashion. The desire for more healthy lifestyles has affected the consumption of fizzy drinks. Low calorie "diet" products are now more popular so a whole new range of brands has sprung up as new competitors for products such as Coca-Cola and Pepsi. They reacted by introducing low calorie versions.

The Risk of Government Regulation

Governments regularly interfere in certain sectors. For example in food and drink, in financial products/services and in utility service supply and distribution. The UK Government has recently imposed a tax on high-sugar soft drinks which has raised the prices or some products and caused some manufacturers to reformulate their products.

> **Point # 19**
>
> Regulation can destroy markets.

Alcoholic drinks are particularly subject to regulation and marketing in some countries is severely restricted. The era of US "Prohibition" in the 1920s was an extreme example.

Medical products are also highly regulated on the grounds of safety, while financial products are regulated often to protect investors from their own foolishness.

One example of financial regulation was the impact on **Plus500** of tougher rules on CFDs by the FCA and European regulators. That caused their share price to drop by over 30% in February 2018. Most investors in CFDs are ignorant speculators and most lose money so it was hardly surprising that the company was vulnerable to more regulation.

Banks are highly regulated following many past failures which wiped out investors' and depositors' money.

Socialist governments have a penchant for more regulation and in the extreme for nationalizing companies with the result that investors in the equity can be wiped out – for example as in the Northern Rock and Bradford & Bingley banks in 2008. At the time of writing a socialist government might threaten utility companies if they came into power in the UK.

Note that Governments are particularly prone to intervene in monopoly or oligopoly situations. Such situations require close monitoring but are usually signaled in some way well in advance.

The Risk of Failure to Develop a New Product

Some new products never get out of the lab. That can apply to almost any product where the science or technology can simply not be made to work and work reliably. It is particularly common with pharmaceutical products where a very high proportion fail in clinical trials or fail to win regulatory approval. This can happen because the product is ineffective or has dangerous side-effects. Only one in ten new drugs actually pass all clinical trials and make it to the market.

> **Point # 20**
>
> Only one in ten new drugs make it to market!

Production Process Risk

Even when a product is in production, technical failures can mean that production has to be halted on safety or other grounds.

44

Extreme examples are nuclear power station explosions in Japan and Russia, but the Bhopal and Seveso chemical disasters were more lethal. Such failures cause the regulatory authorities to shut down production, sometimes permanently.

Mines are also prone to unexpected production problems which can halt production even if there are no human casualties which there often are, e.g. from flooding and explosions.

Risk of Reputation and Brand Damage

Failing products, or dangerous ones, can be disastrous for a company's reputation and make the brand name toxic. The Chevrolet Corvair was one example – a car that would turn over at the drop of hat – or the Ford Pinto that could easily explode if rear-ended. Both products had design defects that could kill you.

But sometimes brands can be damaged through no fault of the company. Tylenol, an OTC drug, was the victim of criminal contamination in 1982 that killed seven people. It was probably an extortion case.

Several similar cases in other products occurred soon after. Social media have provided a new platform for extortion or attacks by disgruntled individuals.

Some of the biggest damage can now occur when IT security is breached and personal information or credit card data is stolen. There have been too many major such breaches to even mention.

The Risk of Management Incompetence

One of the biggest threats to the value of an investment in a company is that the chief executive or chairman is simply incompetent. By over-confidence they can take on too many risks by taking on excessive debt, making dubious acquisitions, failing to build a build a sound management team, and in numerous other ways. The case of the Royal Bank of Scotland was one such example which was covered in Chapter 1.

How do you judge the competence of management? With difficulty is the trite answer mainly because it can take years after a manager is appointed before his mistakes obviously damage a business, and the more senior the role the longer it takes to be revealed. The bigger the company, also the longer it takes.

But a successful track record in previous roles is always worth looking for. If you know something about the sector in which a company operates, for example you may have worked in it yourself, then try to meet the management so you can ask a few questions. Just a few may enable you to judge whether you feel a person is both knowledgeable and experienced.

The Risk of Fraud and False Accounting

Fraud in public companies has been endemic ever since the joint-stock company was invented. It is a particular problem where new companies are being promoted by unscrupulous persons which has been only somewhat moderated by the demands for a prospectus, by changes to the Companies Act and by the Listing Rules. But consider this quotation from the book "The Law and Practice of Joint Stock

> **Point # 21**
>
> Fraud and false accounting are endemic.

Companies Incorporated Under The Companies Acts – 1862 to 1900" by Anthony Pulbrook (4th Edition 1908): "The plain fact is, that the public look upon taking shares in companies as a means of speculating without any trouble to themselves, their principal object is to sell their shares at a profit, hence the majority take little trouble in seeing that the company's affairs are honestly conducted. In fact in all companies it is simply a question of the devil take the hindmost".

A good book on the subject of historic frauds is "White-collar Crime in Modern England – Financial Fraud and Business Morality 1845-1929" published in 1992 which covers a number of cases.

There have been many recent cases of fraudulent companies listing on the AIM market in the UK – for example **Globo**, **Patisserie**, and a number of Chinese AIM listed companies.

But **Polly Peck** was an example of a FTSE-100 company. These companies were not necessarily launched on public markets with the intention that they would be frauds on investors, but subsequently became so because of the temptation in senior executives to inflate profits or a desire to extract non-existent profits.

Banks were particularly vulnerable in the past when it was easy to set them up. Why? Because "that's where the money is" according to the more conventional bank robber Willie Sutton when he was asked why he stole from banks.

Detecting fraud in companies can be very difficult as the accounts are typically dressed up to look "reasonable" to the average investor. Even the cash alleged to be on the balance sheet can prove to be a fiction (e.g. in Globo and Patisserie) even though bank deposits should be verified during audits.

False accounting is often a symptom of aggressive accounting policies and the desire to inflate revenue and profits, or meet targets. **Quindell** was one such example and the **Autonomy/HP** case could be considered to be the same in many respects although it has been turned into a criminal case in the USA. There is often a narrow line between fraud and over-optimistic accounting.

Misleading accounts can often be identified given sufficient time and patience - in other words by good due diligence. But not all investors have the time or inclination to put in the effort. Institutional investors are often victims when they take up placings as they do not have time to do much research and may have limited information. A good book on the subject, recently published is "The Signs Were There" by Tim Steer which covers a number of cases and how the problems could be identified, even if few people did so.

Debt Risk

High debts in a company increase the risk for equity investors. If a company defaults on its debt, then ordinary shareholders are often wiped out by insolvency, administration, or rescues that involve debt for equity swaps that dilute ordinary shareholders out of sight.

The gearing or interest cover in the financial profile of a company are the numbers to look at. But companies typically go bust because they simply run out of cash. Ratios such as the Current Ratio (current assets divided by current liabilities) or the more sophisticated Altman Z-Score can give you a good handle on the risk of failure.

Point # 22

High debt is dangerous.

Debt is dangerous simply because if the market for a company's products or services turns down, or the general economy declines, then the company may be unable to service its debt, i.e. pay the interest or capital when it becomes due.

Debt can be favoured by some companies as opposed to issuing more equity because it can be seen as being cheaper and avoids dilution of existing shareholders. What is an appropriate level of debt depends on the nature of the company. Property companies can have relatively high levels of debt without taking undue risks but early stage technology companies should preferably raise equity finance rather than debt partly because their markets can rapidly change and with few assets against which debt can be secured, debt can be expensive.

Exchange Rate Risk

Many companies are vulnerable to foreign currency exchange rate changes. Importers can suddenly find that they have to pay more in local currency, eroding their profit margins. Exporters may simply find their products are no longer price competitive in foreign markets. Such risks can be hedged against by using forward exchange contracts but often only to a limited extent and at considerable cost. It's worth identifying whether affected companies have hedged against such risks.

Business Acquisition Risk

One of the commonest causes of unexpected corporate problems is where the company makes an acquisition.

Acquisitions are inherently risky and a high proportion turn out to be less successful than anticipated. The bigger the acquisition in relation to the size of the acquiring company, the bigger the risk.

Does a company make sensible acquisitions in businesses that are good strategic fits and relatively small in size, or take big chances? That is a question worth asking.

> **Point # 23**
>
> Acquisitions can be risky.

The merger of **America Online** and **Time Warner** was a good example of a disastrous and misconceived merger. The acquisition by **HP** of **Autonomy** was another example that caused HP to write off $9 billion, i.e. most of the acquisition cost, even if HP was misled by dubious accounting practices with limited due diligence being performed.

Foreign Adventures Risk

A common mistake by management is to underestimate the risk associated with foreign adventures – namely the setting up of new foreign subsidiaries in another country or making an acquisition in another country.

> **Point # 24**
>
> Foreign adventures are risky.

The problem is lack of knowledge of a new market, in a country with a different culture. However much market research one does and even if you hire local staff, you will learn the hard way that the business may not thrive as expected. A good example was **Tesco's** foray into the USA with "Fresh & Easy". In 2007 Tesco launched what was described as a "low risk venture" to open supermarkets on the west coast. They did very extensive market research to support the new store formats, which were innovative rather than copying established competitors. They also had to build two large distribution warehouses after deciding they could not make a profit without "scaling up" the project. By 2013 they had decided to close down the operation and write-off $1.8 billion. In addition to the direct costs, there was clearly an enormous diversion of management time on a non-core business.

The West Coast of the USA is more cosmopolitan in nature than many other parts of the country with an apparent readiness to accept new products and services. It is also of course English speaking. But local shopping habits were ignored with the result that acceptance of the stores never took off.

Retailing is a particularly difficult business to move to another country, perhaps because one is dealing with consumers with long ingrained habits. It is perhaps easier with software or other technology products but it still requires effort to adapt to local standards and customs. English companies have a tendency to consider the USA as home ground due to the common language but they need to bear in mind the alleged comment by George Bernard Shaw that "The United States and Great Britain are two countries separated by a common language".

Even in Europe there are vast differences between countries despite much recent mixing of peoples. Southern Europe and France are particularly problematic and such matters as employment law vary enormously across Europe.

Geographic distances should not be ignored. Beware of any UK companies that wish to move into Japan, China, Australia or the West Coast of the USA. Management intelligence might be eroded by too much jetlag, and the time differences inhibit casual conversations at convenient times.

Take-overs of companies in foreign countries where there is a different culture and language compounds the risks associated with acquisitions.

But all growing and ambitious businesses sooner or later need to expand overseas. The key question is how they go about this. Do they do it without too much expenditure and with patience, or rush into the new venture because they see gold before their eyes?

Point # 25

Foreign adventures should not be rushed.

Controlling Risk & Paranoid Management

Companies face so many risks, and I have only covered a few of them above, that it is extremely important for management to identify the risks they face and try to prevent them crystalizing.

Experience can assist in that regard, but the best managers can be quite paranoid about controlling risk – hence the subtitle of this Chapter – "Only the Paranoid Survive".

The personality of the CEO can give you a hint as to whether they are likely to take more or less risk. Do they appear to be risk takers? For example, do they like extreme sports, drive fast or cycle furiously? Their past careers and profiles in finan-cial/business publications can help to give you some views on their personality.

How a company reacts to a major threat to its business can tell you a lot about the quality and experience of the management. All companies tend to face such threats sooner or later. Do they ignore a threat or take steps to counter it? Do they invest in new products or new services in new markets or continue to reward the loyalty of investors with high dividends when it has long since become inappropriate to do so?

The newspaper industry is a classic example of where income from both customers and advertisers declined as the internet invaded the market for news. Many print newspapers have gone out of business, suffered large financial losses or had to adapt to an on-line service model. It has been a painful process.

Investors need to be wary about investing in companies whose markets are subject to existential change.

Chapter 4 - Investor Checklist

Chapter 4 – Positive Qualities	Tick Here
No major business risks obvious?	
No new competitors apparent?	
Low risk of technological obsolescence?	
Markets not subject to change?	
No risk of Government regulation?	
No risk of product development failure?	
Little risk of process failure?	
Low risk of reputation/brand damage?	
Management judged competent?	
Low risk of fraud/false accounting?	
Low debt?	
Low exposure to exchange rate risk?	
Few business acquisitions?	
No foreign adventures?	
Are the management risk averse?	

Chapter 5

Rational Pricing and Good Margins

"The single most important decision in evaluating a business is pricing power... If you've got the power to raise prices without losing business to a competitor, you've got a very good business. And if you have to have a prayer session before raising the price by 10 percent, then you've got a terrible business"...........Warren Buffett.

For any business, rational pricing is one key to generating profits. Maximizing prices and revenue is extremely important for any business. Research indicates that a 1% improvement in revenue typically creates an 11% improvement in operating profit. Therefore price optimization can have a very significant impact on the bottom line (M. Mam and R. Rosiello, Harvard Business Review, Sept 1992).

Having pricing power is a function of brand loyalty, barriers to entry and other aspects covered in previous chapters. Pricing power helps but often companies do not maximise their revenue and profitability by paying little attention to how they set their product or service pricing. Such companies might use cost-plus pricing to achieve what they consider reasonable margins when they might be better off using value-based pricing, i.e. pricing their products based on the value they are giving to their customers, not what it costs to produce them.

> **Point # 26**
>
> Price optimization is important.

I covered the whole subject of pricing extensively in a chapter of my book "Beware the Zombies" – see:
https://www.roliscon.com/books.html

Creating and Maintaining Good Margins

Selling prices of products may be determined by what the market will bear, but margins are determined by the difference between sales prices and the cost of purchasing or production. Businesses operating on low margins are extremely vulnerable to economic trends and competitor challenges. You should always look at the overall operating margins of a company before investing. Creating and maintaining adequate margins are extremely important.

The author first learned that when I worked for a retailing company when the CEO asked me to program one of the then new programmable calculators so he could get an instant fix on the likely margins on carpets when negotiating with suppliers.

Margins can vary dependent on the nature of the business. For example, supermarkets typically have very low margins which is compensated for by the volume of sales and hence profits that are generated as a result – Tesco has an operating margin of 2.9% at the time of writing. But for most good businesses operating margins should be 10% or higher. Operating margins are a very good indication of whether a business has pricing power or not.

High margins often enable high returns on capital to be achieved in a business – one of the defining qualities of a good company so far as investors are concerned.

Chapter 5 - Investor Checklist

Chapter 5 – Positive Qualities	Tick Here
Prices rationally set?	
High margins?	

Chapter 6

Company Culture, Structure & Pay

"Corporate culture is the only sustainable competitive advantage that is completely within the control of the entrepreneur"...........David Cummings, Pardot

Company culture is a major differentiator between companies but its influence is not always obvious at first glance. Having an appropriate culture to the market in which the company operates is very important to business success, but there are some aspects that are common to all companies.

An Appropriate Culture

Companies can have different approaches to doing business and the culture can change over time. New businesses tend to be created by entrepreneurs who have taken risks and formed a new company so as to be independent and escape from big company bureaucracy. Their mental approach will influence the business and they are likely to take risks to achieve success.

But when a business grows in size it needs a different leadership style and more bureaucracy. An academic study showed that firms led by the people who founded them were 9.4% less productive, on average, and on average had consistently lower management scores—which typically rose once the founder-CEO was replaced. To quote: "Founder CEOs were by far

Point # 27

Founder CEOs are the worst.

the worst type of CEO," said Victor Bennett, an assistant professor of strategy at Duke's Fuqua School of Business and a co-author of the paper.

The problem often arises because a company founder can be a very dominant personality in a company and hence can ignore advice from others or ignore changes in the market place by repeating what worked in the past.

Henry Ford at **Ford Motor Company** is one example, or recent examples might be Mark Zuckerberg at **Facebook** who initially ignored privacy concerns or Elon Musk at **Tesla** who is a typical entrepreneur now leading a large auto company – at least it is of a size where it needs a large and experienced management team but building that does not seem to be one of his strengths. Tesla is a public company but Elon suggested it might be taken private in 2018 – perhaps to escape concerns about regulatory compliance and corporate governance.

The more complex the company, and the more rapidly changing the technology or markets, the sooner founders tend to come unstuck. But in simpler, more traditional companies, founders can be successful for a long time – for example in retailers such as Jack Cohen at **Tesco.**

But founders who develop a more delegated management or collegiate management style in complex technology businesses can be more successful. Consider the example of Bill Hewlett and Dave Packard at **Hewlett-Packard**, but even there the company had some difficulties after the retirement of the founders with a succession of CEO changes and business issues – the company has subsequently split in two.

Founders and Succession

Founders can remain at the helm of companies long after they should have given way to others. This is even so in public companies even if the board or shareholders have in theory the power to remove them – the fact that they still often own a large proportion of the shares and have often appointed "yes men (or women)" to the board who are unlikely to challenge them thwarts any change.

One question to ask for investors is: Is a founder still in charge and if so does that create a risk?

A long-standing and successful CEO, even if not a founder, can likewise become a dominant person and in that case the questions might be: a) have they become over-confident? and b) Is there a clear succession?

Take the example of Ian MacLaurin (now Lord MacLaurin) at **Tesco.** He joined the board of Tesco as Managing Director in 1970 after a long career with the company. Under his leadership it became the largest UK retailer and he became Chairman in 1985. He retired in 1997. But his successors oversaw a disastrous venture in the USA and a subsequent accounting scandal.

Point # 28	There is clearly a risk associated with successions from dominant and highly successful CEOs. One particular danger is when CEOs
Dominant CEOs are dangerous.	move to Chairman (as MacLaurin did). That is no longer seen as wise corporate governance as it perpetuates the dominance of the individual.

Beware over-dominant CEOs in general. The example of Fred Goodwin at the **Royal Bank of Scotland**, who embarked on a risky business strategy which eventually led to a disastrous acquisition, shows how a forceful personality can be very dangerous for investors. Strong leadership can be a positive business advantage but it can go too far.

Humble personalities can be much better business leaders. The book "Good to Great" by Jim Collins covers what turns good businesses into great ones and the profiles of the leaders who achieve that. He describes how some of them had a "compelling modesty" in always assigning the success of the business to others. They are typically "quiet, humble, modest, reserved, shy, gracious, mild-mannered, self-effacing, understated... and so forth" he says. But what they are good at is building a good team of managers.

The CEOs who are brash, outspoken and love publicity are some of the most dangerous for investors. In small companies they can often be persuasive speakers and lead investors to invest in their companies on the basis of the future prospects. But the reality is often more prosaic.

Executive Chairmen

Combining the roles of Chief Executive and Chairman is a positive danger. Would the fraud at **Patisserie** have been discovered earlier if Luke Johnson had not been both CEO and Chairman? That's apart from his multiple other business roles and activities, plus other possible danger signs were his high public profile and forceful personality.

This is what FT journalist Sarah Gordan had to say on the failings in the City: "One reason **Lehman** went under was because it was run by a joint chairman and chief executive who, by 2008, had accrued almost total dominion, and who was not held to account by those with a duty to do so. Dick Fuld's board members neither delved deeply enough into the real activities of the bank, nor did they challenge the person running it sufficiently. Being on the Lehman board, it seemed, was a social honour rather than a fiduciary responsibility" (FT March 2019).

Executive Chairman are of course positively discouraged by the UK Corporate Governance Code but there are still a lot of them in public companies. They can get by on the "comply or explain" rule where justification is not difficult. Such reasons as "the need to retain their valuable experience" are commonplace.

> **Point # 29**
>
> Executive Chairmen should be avoided

The only sound reason for an Executive Chairman is when a company is facing dire difficulties, needs forceful management to survive and where prompt action (with little debate) is essential. This is equivalent to when the Roman Republic appointed a "Dictator" with absolute powers to face a military emergency and who had powers greater than the consuls and tribunes. Dictators could be appointed for specific time periods and were obliged to resign after their task was accomplished – both wise restrictions.

Company Structure

How a company is structured should be appropriate to its size and marketplace. Young entrepreneurial companies tend to have "loose" structures which can adapt rapidly to changes.

More mature companies have more hierarchical structures as their structure becomes more formalized over time. The question investors have to ask is "does the company have an appropriate structure?" Has it outgrown its initial model and need to change? Do the management delegate enough or too little? Is there over-reliance on a few key individuals?

Investors need to be wary about companies that have a sprawling structure, diverse operating businesses or multiple joint ventures where they do not have a controlling interest. Such companies are called "conglomerates" and were very popular in the 1960s partly due to the fact that acquisition accounting was lax and profits could be engineered simply by making multiple acquisitions. A classic example was US business **Ling-Temco-Vought** (later LTV Corporation) that had interests in aerospace, electronics, cabling, meat packing, sporting goods, pharmaceuticals, airlines, car rental and holiday resorts. By 1969 it had purchased 33 companies but the profits of the parent company grew slower than the individual companies it had purchased and it also ran into anti-trust legal problems. It filed for bankruptcy protection in 1986.

Since that time investors have tended to look negatively at companies that comprise multiple operating businesses with little obvious synergy between them and will often push for a break-up into their component parts because frequently the individual companies can be valued in total at more than the parent. A recent example is **Whitbread** whose two main operations were Premier Inns and Costa Coffee. The latter has now been sold off.

But there are some conglomerates that do manage the diversity successfully. **Berkshire Hathaway** is one example. Delegated management appears to be the key, with only central financial targets being imposed.

Motivated and Happy Staff

Good managers provide clear leadership and ensure that staff are happy and well-motivated. This is particularly essential for the middle-management in a company who have the most influence on its success.

Are the management consumed by internal politics, by inability to get decisions from their leaders, by concerns about their future jobs, or lack trust in their leaders? These questions are not often easy to answer but talking to employees of a company can give you some insight. If you attend AGMs of companies it is often the case that you will meet newly retired employees who still hold shares who are often willing to talk openly about the business and its management.

Fine words but do they mean anything? Many Annual Reports contain comments about the commitment of the company to their employees. For example, this is a paragraph in the Annual Report of **Safestore**, a FTSE-250 self-storage company, in 2019: "IIP (Investors in People) recognized that the business continues to undergo significant self-review in order to create a sustainable organization with an unwavering commitment to improve performance through people. It is also recognized that the levels of pride in the Company are high and what sets the Company apart is the culture of being friendly, supportive and showing a genuine interest in the individual". This makes for good public relations but it may not mean a lot in practice. But it is undoubtedly the case that companies with a paternalistic attitude to their staff often do better than others in the long-term. If employees are happy, they may communicate this to the company's customers with a positive impact on sales and customer satisfaction.

Environmental, Social and Governance (ESG)

One of the more recent focuses for investors, particularly institutional fund managers looking to differentiate their offering, is how well a company performs on environment, social and governance (ESG) criteria.

A report by Axioma in 2018 suggested that high ESG scores correlated in large and medium sized companies with outperformance over the previous four years. Boston Consulting Group also reported that companies with more ethical operations made bigger profits according to the Financial Times.

Note that Governance issues are covered in more detail in a later Chapter.

Ethically Sound?

One of the conundrums that all investors face is whether to invest in companies that potentially damage the health of the public directly, or indirectly via environmental damage. Should you invest in tobacco companies, in oil/gas companies, in coal companies, in gambling companies or a myriad of other question-able businesses?

Many such companies are large companies with a long history and because of their "mature" nature often pay exceptionally high dividends. They are therefore often appealing investments to retirees looking for income. But what really matters is the total return from investing in them, and the risks they might face in future. All such companies face high regulatory risks. Coal and oil/gas producers might be put out of business by public concerns about their activities and sooner, or later, Government imposing severe restrictions on them.

Some ethically challenged businesses are relatively new – for example, internet gaming companies and payday loan companies.

> **Point # 30**
>
> Ethically challenged businesses should be avoided.

The author had an investment in a payments company whose customers were mainly those betting on-line in the USA. The US Congress added to the Safe Port Act in 2006 - the Unlawful Internet Gambling Enforcement Act (UIGEA) – at the very last minute and without any notice. The company only narrowly avoided going out of business as half its revenue disappeared.

In general, ethically dubious businesses, or those that run close to the law, should be avoided. Some investors will argue that the profits that can be achieved in such businesses offset the risks, but in reality investors are often not aware of the real risks and such companies rarely fully disclose them to investors.

Remuneration

Overpaid Chief Executives, Chairmen and other directors are a warning sign. As mentioned above, many of the most successful CEOs are humble people. They have low expectations for their own remuneration.

But pay of senior executives has been ramping up in recent years despite public concerns, and increased regulation. This has been driven by generous bonus and Long-Term Incentive Plans (LTIPs) often paying many multiples of base salaries.

But do aggressive incentive schemes produce better performance? The answer is no according to several academic studies. Senior managers do not work harder if paid more, and having a juicy carrot dangled in front of them some years in the future makes no difference.

> **Point # 31**
>
> High director pay does not result in superior company performance.

In fact, they can produce the negative result that a highly competent CEO can receive so much in bonuses in just a few years that they can retire and the company loses his or her skills.

Another problem is that aggressive bonus schemes can encourage risky behaviour in senior managers. This became a particular concern after the failure of banks in the financial crisis of 2008-9. In such companies it often appeared to be a one-way bet for the managers in that high bonuses were combined with high basic salaries. But if the business bets failed, they still kept their jobs, or the LTIPs were reset.

If pay is high at the top of an organisation, then high pay tends to trickle down to lower levels thereby increasing the total wage bill of a company. If it does not the gulf between senior management and the lower paid can become excessively wide, which demotivates more junior staff.

ShareSoc (the UK Individual Shareholders Society) has published Remuneration Guidelines for both Smaller and Larger Companies which are worth studying if you have doubts about what a company is paying. Smaller companies might justify performance-related share option schemes on the basis that they cannot afford the cash required to pay high salaries or short-term bonuses, but in larger companies there is no such excuse. One of the author's most successful investments was in a company (**Delcam**) where shareholders at an AGM once suggested the directors should pay themselves more. But that does not happen very often!

When looking at a company as a potential; investment, the following approach is suggested:

a) Read the comments of the Remuneration Committee Chairman in the Annual Report to see if there is anything of note.

b) Review the quantum of pay for the two highest paid directors (which for UK companies is easy now there is a "single figure audited remuneration" table). Is it reasonable in relation to the size and profitability of the company? Any figure over £1 million, regardless of the size of the company, I would suggest is unreasonable.

c) Similarly, any company where pay has gone up while profits and/or dividends have gone down should be viewed negatively.

d) The pay of non-executives I would also glance at.

e) Look at the LTIPs (which are generally questionable anyway) and bonus schemes. Any of those that enable more than 100% of basic pay to be achieved should be viewed with suspicion.

It is unfortunately the case in the modern business environment that you will not find many companies that meet the criteria given above. The key questions to ask are is the pay outrageously high? Or is it well above other similar companies are paying? If the answer to either question is "Yes" then you should not invest in it.

Flash Offices and Excessive Perks

Largesse with company cars, private jets, apartments and other perks for senior management are a definite warning sign that you should not invest.

Consider the case of **Petrofac**, an oil services company. In 2013 it was revealed that it had spent over $1.5 million on a private jet for it's CEO and similar sums in previous years. The Annual Report of the company hardly made it clear that he was the prime beneficiary. The company subsequently suffered from an investigation by the Serious Fraud Office (SFO) over bribery allegations and at the time of writing legal action has been announced by solicitors acting on behalf of shareholders who have lost billions on their investments in the company. Petrofac share price peaked at 1750p in 2012 but is now only 390p.

Another negative sign is when a company is seen to be spending excessive amounts on their facilities, on corporate sponsorship or entertaining clients.

The regime of Fred Goodwin at RBS was another good example of hedonism in top management.

If you get the opportunity to visit a company's premises (e.g. for an AGM) then this is a good opportunity to see their operations. Premises should be good quality but not luxurious. You may also get the opportunity to see the company cars parked in the car park.

Chapter 6 - Investor Checklist

Chapter 6 – Positive Qualities	Tick Here
Appropriate culture?	
Founders no longer running the business?	
Independent chairman?	
Appropriate corporate structure?	
Motivated and happy staff?	
Rate highly on ESG measures?	
Reasonable remuneration for directors?	
Not too generous with perks?	

Chapter 7

Company Regulation and Governance

"Every right implies a responsibility; Every opportunity, an obligation; Every possession, a duty"....
John D. Rockefeller.

The way a company operates and the regulations it adheres to have a large influence on the outcome of any investment. That includes the activities of the directors.

Company Domicile

Where a company is registered is definitely worth checking because it affects the laws under which the company operates. Even in those more developed countries with stronger traditions of protecting investors, e.g. the USA, you may find that there are differences between states. Delaware is generally viewed as more friendly to companies and their management than to their investors.

UK listed companies whose operating base is overseas may not be subject to the Takeover Panel Code (an important protection for minority shareholders), and can often create legal difficulties when wrong-doing needs to be pursued.

It is unfortunately a fact of life that some countries are viewed as protecting investors better than others. For example, when problems with Chinese AIM companies arose in recent years, many investors found it was difficult to enforce their rights in law or take action against errant directors.

In general, for UK listed companies, any domicile outside the UK adds to the risk of investing in a company. Domicile in the Channel Islands or Isle of Man is also not ideal.

Applicable Listing Rules

In addition to the Articles of a Company and the UK Companies Act, the actions of a publicly listed company and its directors are governed by Listing Rules. These are different for main market UK companies as opposed to AIM companies with the former being more onerous and rigorous. AIM companies are regulated by the LSE, a private organisation, while main market companies are regulated by the Financial Conduct Authority (FCA). There is a difference in the standard of regulation, and in enforcement, between the two.

AIM company shares are generally seen as being riskier investments because of that difference but also because they are often smaller in size, with a shorter track record when first listed.

The Listing Rules, whether a main market or AIM company, require the publication via a Regulatory News Announcement (RNS) of news about a company – particularly price sensitive information, i.e. news that might affect the share price. Companies and their directors who fail to disclose all relevant information promptly and accurately should be avoided.

Corporate Governance Code

The Listing Rules for main market public companies in the UK require such companies to explain how they have applied the principles in the Corporate Governance Code in their Annual Reports. Similar codes have been adopted in many other countries. The Financial Reporting Council (FRC) is responsible for maintaining and publishing the UK Code. Here is a summary of the main points and what is covered:

▪ Board leadership should ensure an effective and entrepreneurial board, that the company has the necessary resources to meet its objectives and effectively measure performance against them. The board should engage with shareholders and other stakeholders, including the workforce, to ensure long-term sustainable success.

- The Chair should lead the board and there should be an appropriate combination of executive and non-executive directors with no dominance by one individual or group. The Chair should be independent and there should be a majority of independent non-executive directors.

- There should be a "senior" independent non-executive director to act as an intermediary to the Chair for shareholders and other directors.

- A nomination committee should be established with a majority of independent non-executive directors. The committee should ensure succession planning. Directors who have served for more than 9 years are not to be considered "independent" and Chairs should not serve for more than 9 years.

- The board should establish an audit committee of independent non-executive directors. They should monitor the integrity of financial statements and review internal financial controls and audit functions (both internal and external). They have responsibility to recommend the appointment of external auditors.

- The board should explain the principal risks the company faces in the Annual Report, and monitor those risks.

- The board should establish a remuneration committee of independent non-executive directors which will determine the policy for executive director and senior management remuneration, plus the Chair. There are specific rules on remuneration to support alignment with long-term shareholder interests and good practice.

What does "independent" mean when referring to directors? In summary it means not being a former employee (e.g. executive director), not having a business relationship with the company, not having close family ties with the company or its advisers or employees, not representing a major shareholder and not having served on the board for more than 9 years.

This is designed to ensure that all directors take decisions on a rational basis, not from personal motives and do not develop too cosy a relationship with the executives.

Note that the principles in the Code have helped to ensure that the worst abuses seen in the past (as perceived by investors) are avoided, but it is by no means a perfect system, particularly as feeble explanations can sometimes be given for non-adherence.

As pointed out in a previous chapter, Executive Chairmen are still common, particularly in smaller companies. Similarly the independence of non-executive directors is often questioned, and many stay in the role too long, i.e. they remain longer than the recommended nine years – this is a particular problem in investment companies (i.e. investment trusts).

Some directors consider adherence to a corporate governance code as a "box-ticking" exercise as they often call it, but the reality is that it can have a very profound impact on the way a company operates. That is particularly so when a company runs into financial or other difficulties.

> **Point # 32**
>
> Adherence to a corporate governance code may have a big impact.

Companies listed on the AIM market of the London Stock Exchange are technically "unlisted" so far as the Companies Act and associated regulations are concerned. But they are "traded" companies and so are still covered by some regulations such as the Companies (Shareholder Rights) Regulations. However they are not bound by the UK Corporate Governance Code.

Prior to 2018, there was no obligation for AIM companies to adhere to any governance code but the AIM listing rules were then changed to require them to identity a governance code they would be following – still on a "comply or explain" basis.

Many AIM companies have chosen to adopt the Quoted Companies Alliance (QCA) governance code. The QCA represents small and medium sized companies. Its code is more limited in scope than the UK Corporate Governance Code.

(Note: ShareSoc provides a guide on the UK corporate governance and regulatory environment on its web site where some of the above text was previously published).

Large or Small Director Share Stakes

Common abuses of corporate governance codes happen when one or more directors have a controlling stake in the business, i.e. own more than 50% of the equity. Even owning 40% usually means they can win any vote and effectively have control.

One danger of such large stakes is that they might be tempted to take a company private if they think the shares are undervalued or they are simply fed up with sticking to the rules required of public companies.

On the other hand, it is important for directors to have a significant interest in a company's shares so as to align their interests with that of other shareholders. Having a substantial interest provides a powerful incentive to promote the success of the company. This particularly applies to executive directors but even non-executive directors should have a non-trivial shareholding. It's even better if the directors acquired their share stakes by purchasing shares in the market rather than simply being a beneficiary of nil-price share option scheme awards.

Point # 33

Share stakes should be not too large and not too small.

Share stakes of directors should be big enough to be meaningful and to provide good incentives but not so large that they can dominate the board and other shareholders.

Director Share Sales and Purchases

The transactions in the shares of a company by the directors are always published in RNS announcements. Substantial share sales by directors with no obvious good reason are a warning sign.

Share purchases, particularly by non-executive directors other than soon after their appointment, are a positive sign.

Too Many Directors

Large FTSE-100 companies can have as many as 20 directors. This can make board meetings quite dysfunctional, and lead to dominance by the Chairman or CEO. With so many directors, some of them are not going to be saying much.

Too Many Jobs

Where the non-executive directors have multiple roles in other companies, it often leads to poor oversight of the affairs of a company. This problem is called "overboarding". Directors need sufficient time and energy in order to be effective representatives of shareholders' interests.

Point # 34

Overboarding is a known problem.

Non-executive directors should not have more than five such roles, and company chairmen should not chair multiple companies. The larger the company, the more important it is for Chairmen to have the required time to look after it.

Would **Patisserie** have collapsed into administration in 2018 if Luke Johnson had not had over 25 directorships at the time, apart from also writing a column for a national newspaper?

AGMs – When, Where and Well Run?

A good indication of how much attention a board of directors takes to the interests of minority shareholders is the conduct of the Annual General Meeting.

If a meeting is held in a remote part of the country, or even overseas, at inconvenient times, that suggests that the directors do not wish to have shareholders attend. It's also a good way to avoid having to answer questions.

Point # 35

Is the company AGM well run and questions answered?

Directors can avoid answering questions in other ways, even though there is a legal obligation to do so. They can claim business confidentiality, the obligations of non-disclosure agreements, or simple ignorance about the answer. As with politicians, some company directors are experts in avoiding responding to straight questions with simple answers. Investing in companies where the CEO or Chairman is of that ilk should be avoided.

ShareSoc published a document written by the author of this book in 2013 entitled "How to Run a General Meeting of a Public Company" which gives guidance on what investors should expect. It goes into more detail on this subject. See:
https://www.sharesoc.org/How_To_Run_General_Meetings.pdf

Prejudicial Share Placings

A good indication of how much attention a company pays to the interests of minority investors is when they issue new shares. In larger companies this may be via a rights issue where all share-holders can participate. However heavily discounted rights issues are a positive danger sign.

In smaller companies it is common practice to do a "placing". This can be justified on the grounds of necessary speed (e.g. for an acquisition) or expense, but if it is at a substantial discount to the previous market price (i.e. more than 10%), that is a very negative sign.

Any past record of doing such discounted placings should rule the company out as an investment unless there was an "open offer" option included. Otherwise existing investors are being diluted and value transferred to the new investors. Past share placings can be picked up easily by reviewing past RNS announcements.

Point # 36

Look at past share placings.

Share Buy-Backs

Companies with more cash on their balance sheet than they need in the short-term may undertake market purchases of their shares, commonly called buy-backs. The alternatives are to pay special dividends or undertake tender offers. The justification given for buy-backs is that the shares are undervalued and that it will enhance earnings per share by using the cash in this way. But judging whether the shares are undervalued is not easy and most directors are unable to take an unbiased view on that matter.

Buy-backs are often in the interests of directors because performance bonuses are frequently based on earnings per share and can be inflated without adjustment by buy-backs.

Point # 37

Companies that do share buy-backs are often pursuing a dubious financial strategy.

A company that has no use for the cash other than to buy back its shares is effectively saying that it cannot identify a good use of the money in terms of future investment projects or acquisitions, i.e. it cannot get a satisfactory return on the money and hence might be best to return it to shareholders. Such companies are those that are clearly going downhill rather than expanding and are not likely to make good investments.

It is unfortunately the case that many larger companies have got into the habit of undertaking regular market buy-backs of late, even in preference to reducing their debt.

One exception as regards the merits of buy-backs is investment trusts (closed-end investment companies), where buying back shares at a discount to net asset value is rational. Indeed in venture capital trusts (VCTs) sometimes the company is the only buyer of shares and without them there is no liquidity and discounts can reach very large levels.

Share Liquidity and Bid/Offer Spreads

Smaller companies may have little liquidity in their shares, i.e. there is little share trading volume each day. This not just leads to volatility in the share price, as just one or two trades of any size can move the price, but also leads to wide bid/offer spreads (the difference between the prices on offer for buying and selling shares). Any bid/offer spread (sometimes called the bid/ask spread) of more than 5% in smaller companies should be looked on with concern.

Speculative Interest and Too Much Discussion

In smaller companies, such as AIM listed stocks, there can be a high level of speculative interest, i.e. investors who are buying and selling the stock with the objective of making a short-term gain in hours, days or weeks. That's opposed to investors who are buying and holding them for a long-term return. Short-term speculators can react to share price movements rather than fundamental news so that the share prices can rise and fall in waves. For example, they buy when others are buying and sell when others are selling.

Point # 38

Is a company beloved by speculators? If so it should be avoided.

Shares in such companies are open to market abuse by share rampers and shorters where they spread positive and negative comments with the objective of achieving a profit by timing their own share trades to maximise their profits, e.g. buying before "puffing" the stock, and selling after it has reached a peak.

It is a fact that a good indication of the level of speculation in a stock can be deduced by the amount of discussion of it on investment bulletin boards and in tip sheets. Otherwise look at the daily volume of share trades in the company in relation to its market cap.

Legal Disputes?

Any substantial legal disputes that a company is involved in are a negative sign. They should be declared in the Annual Report.

Large Pension Liabilities?

Does a company have major obligations under its pension scheme, i.e. does it run one or more defined benefit schemes which are under-funded in relation to future liabilities? Companies have been moving away from defined benefit schemes to defined contribution schemes but some companies still have big deficits on past defined benefit schemes. For example **BT Plc** had a deficit of £14 billion in 2018. The size of the deficit can swing wildly depending on actuarial life expectancy figures and investment returns, but deficits sooner or later need to be reduced. That may require very substantial extra funding by the company that can wipe out profits. Pensions liabilities should be obvious from reading the Annual Report.

Have You Read the Annual Report?

Both the pensions and legal disputes issues mentioned above emphasise the importance of investors reading the Annual Report of a company before investing in it.

Directors Acting in Your Interests or Theirs?

Many of the points raised in this Chapter and the previous one, help to indicate whether the directors of a company are acting in your interest or their own.

For example, high director pay detracts from profits available to ordinary shareholders, and sets a bad example for other employees. Share buy-backs may increase their bonus pay-outs while directors often participate in discounted share placings.

This problem of directors of companies acting in their interest rather than the owners of a company is known as the "agency problem". Agents acting on behalf of owners of assets may pursue their interests rather than the owners. Corporate governance rules are designed to protect against that but it is not a foolproof solution – just look at the way director pay has ramped up in recent years.

Point # 39

Do you trust the directors to act in your interests?

You may get some hints and the question to ask yourself is "Do you trust the directors to act in your interests?"

Chapter 7 - Investor Checklist

Chapter 7 – Positive Qualities	Tick Here
UK or US domicile?	
Subject to UK Takeover Panel Code?	
Adhere to corporate governance code?	
Large director stakes, but not too large?	
All directors have big shareholdings?	
Not too many directors?	
Directors do not have too many roles?	
Past prejudicial share placings?	
AGMs at convenient time & place?	
AGMs well run?	
Past prejudicial share placings?	
Share buy-backs being used?	
Liquid shares with low bid/offer spread?	
Too much speculative interest?	
No big legal disputes?	
No big pension liabilities?	
You have read the Annual Report?	
Directors can be trusted?	

Chapter 8

Presentation of Accounts

"We won't buy into companies where someone's talking about EBITDA. If you look at all companies, and split them into companies that use EBITDA as a metric and those that don't, I suspect you'll find a lot more fraud in the former group"...... Warren Buffett.

This book argues that financial numbers are not the most important aspect when looking at new companies in which to invest. But how the numbers are presented is certainly important and reflects upon the attitudes of the management.

EBITDA or Not?

There are standards as to how companies can report their financial numbers, commonly labelled "reported figures" in the media. These take into account many aspects which some managements would prefer to ignore. In that case they instead refer to Earnings Before Interest, Taxes, Depreciation and Amortization (EBITDA).

Interest is the interest paid on debt, depreciation is the write down of the capital value of fixed assets while amortization is the write down of intangible assets (e.g. goodwill acquired on an acquisition). Fixed assets such as machinery tend to wear out so do need replacing. Hence it is a definite cost to a business that should be reflected in the profit & loss statement, or as Warren Buffett said "Does management think the tooth fairy pays for capital expenditures?". Ignoring depreciation overstates the profits being generated in a business.

The contrary argument is that EBITDA is a better measure of the operational performance of a business. Private equity investors tend to use EBITDA and multiples thereof to judge the valuation of a business, perhaps because they expect to refinance it.

But it also results in such investors loading up companies with debt that can act as a drag on future performance.

EBITDA is also favored by technology companies such as software businesses who often have large amounts of capitalized development expenditure on their balance sheets. When it was capitalized the development cost effectively disappeared from the relevant period's profits and loss statement, but it is a real cost and should not be ignored.

> **Point # 40**
>
> Using EBITDA can ignore real costs that have been incurred.

Note: this author is not opposed to the capitalization of software development costs as required by accounting standards, but to ignore the amortization of those costs so that they disappear from the financial figures is not appropriate.

Interest payable and taxes payable are definitely a real cost that businesses must pay so it seems even odder to exclude those. EBITDA can be used to compare companies operating under different tax regimes or with different financial structures, but "reported" figures are a better measure for most investors.

Exceptional Items and Adjusted Profits

Many companies report "Exceptional", or "Extraordinary" items (there is no difference in the IFRS standard) in their accounts and exclude them so as to report a "adjusted", "normalized" or "underlying" profit figure. This is on the principle that such items are truly outside the normal course of business and won't be repeated. For example, a major restructuring of a business with high staff redundancy costs might be treated as such.

> **Point # 41**
>
> Beware repeated exceptional items.

But often one sees a company repeatedly use such excuses for failing to achieve their anticipated profits in a year. Investors should be very suspicious about companies that report substantial exceptional items every year.

Sometimes such exceptional items are combined with EBITDA figures and the exclusion of share-based payments to executives to produce "Adjusted EBITDA" and "Adjusted EPS" or "Normalized EPS" (earnings per share). In such cases it can be simpler to look at the cash flows in the business to get a better understanding of the financial trends.

Just Eat is a company that prefers to talk about adjusted EBITDA but complicates matters further by using the name uEBITDA – or underlying EBITDA. There is not even a consistent nomenclature in use and the Financial Reporting Council (FRC) who lay down the rules on how accounts should be published does not seem to be concerned about this.

Financial analysts often prefer to work in normalized figures so as to exclude exceptional years. Figures on forecast earnings supplied by investment platforms are often on that basis. Unfortunately there is no common standard for what is or is not included. Likewise adjusted figures reported in the Annual Reports of companies have the same problem – only the "reported" figures in the statements of comprehensive income and financial position are legally standardized at the time of writing.

The above discussion refers to profits and earnings, but sometimes one sees it extended to other items such as "adjusted revenue" or "adjusted cash". You thought cash was the cash held by a company in its current/deposit bank accounts or in readily marketable securities? But sometimes companies like to include some other things in it. Such sophistry should be viewed with suspicion.

But investors need to be wary because cash on the balance sheet does not necessarily mean it is readily available to be used by the company. It might include client funds – for example a quick look at the balance sheet of payments company **FairFX** for the year ending 2017 shows cash of £51.9 million. You have to look in the Notes where it is reported that £34.1 million of that is actually segregated client funds. Cash nominally available might not be for a wide variety of reasons such as being part of regulatory capital or being held to satisfy the cost of an acquisition.

Examples of Adjustments – GSK & Rolls-Royce

In some companies the difference between the IFRS reported figures and the adjusted figures is not large, but in others they are very different. For example in the 2017 year, **GlaxoSmithKline** reported IFRS Earnings Per Share (EPS) of 31p but "adjusted" EPS of 112p. Clearly the company might prefer to report adjusted figures which is what they mainly talk about in the Annual Report. In the two previous years the two numbers were also quite different, with 2015 being different in the reverse direction. There was not quite so much emphasis on the "Core" figures in that year's Annual Report – they subsequently renamed "Core" to "Adjusted" which at least removed some confusion.

Here is what GSK say about their adjustments in the 2017 report:

"Adjusted results now exclude the following items from Total results: amortisation and impairment of intangible assets (excluding computer software) and goodwill; major restructuring costs, including those costs following material acquisitions; significant legal charges (net of insurance recoveries) and expenses on the settlement of litigation and government investigations, transaction-related accounting adjustments for significant acquisitions, and other items, including disposals of associates, products and businesses and other operating income other than royalty income, together with the tax effects of all of these items and the impact of the enactment of the US Tax Cuts and Jobs Act in 2017.

GSK believes that Adjusted results are more representative of the performance of the Group's operations and allow the key trends and factors driving that performance to be more easily and clearly identified by shareholders."

That's a lot of "Adjustments" in essence, and note that their definition changed from the previous year as some legal costs are now excluded (such costs were very significant in past years due to patent disputes). But are not legal costs in a pharmaceutical company a normal part of doing business that will recur every year? To suggest they are not underlying and on-going costs may surely not be appropriate.

Rolls-Royce is another company that likes to quote underlying figures. In this case even the revenue figure was adjusted down in 2017 from £16.3 billion to £15.1 billion. This is their explanation for the need for that adjustment:

"Underlying revenue is used as it reflects the impact of our foreign exchange (FX) hedging policy by valuing foreign currency revenue at the actual exchange rates achieved as a result of settling FX contracts in the year. This provides a clearer measure of the year-on-year performance."

Rolls-Royce also confuses investors by putting both the underlying operating profit (£1.2 billion) and the reported profit (£4.2 billion) on the face of the Consolidated Income Statement. In addition they give an "alternative view" in Note 1 of the accounts in respect of RRSA contracts (Risk and Revenue Sharing Agreements) which affects both profit figures.

Many companies exclude share option charges from underlying profits for no good reason but **4Imprint** decided in 2018 to include them and restated their previous year's figures accordingly. Perhaps they previously thought that share option charges should not be included in accounts as they used not to be, but they are a real cost on shareholders. In addition, they tend to be present every year so are hardly exceptional.

Adjustments Made in the Accounts of Banks

Annual reports of banks and other financial organizations are typically horrific examples of excessive adjustments and opaque reports.

> **Point # 42**
>
> The accounts of banks can be very opaque.

This is what Chris Boxall had to say in March 2019 in an Investors Champion Podcast on bank accounts: "Exceptionally complicated and full of exceptional comments and exceptional write-offs – you have to wade through hundreds of adjustments". He also said "All these adjustments are a hit to shareholders and should be spelled out" and "If there are lots of adjustments, that is often a red flag".

Note that the Annual Report for **HSBC** in 2018 was 322 pages in length. Banks also for some years have reported costs for mis-selling clients as exceptional, and other legal costs, when it could be argued that this has been part of the normal, and now expected business activity. They are certainly costs borne by shareholders.

Confusing Accounts Confuse Investors

You can see there is enormous variety in how financial figures are reported. Investors might be hopelessly confused by the way the aforementioned companies present their accounts. If they are not confused, they will need extra time to get an understanding of the accounts. Most stock market investors are busy people and it's easy for them to miss important information if the accounts are difficult to understand.

Prudent, Understandable and Consistent

In reality we have a situation where companies vary on what they consider adjustments, and can change the definition from year to year at the whim of the directors. This does not help investors.

Some investors have given up on using what a company reports and choose to make their own adjustments to the IFRS numbers.

The key questions investors need to ask themselves are:

1) Are the "adjustments" to create the underlying numbers reasonable and prudent? In particular are the exceptional items really exceptional, or do they recur every year or could otherwise be a normal and expected cost in the market in which the company operates?

2) Are the adjustments understandable and the information clearly present in preliminary results announcements, half-year announcements and the Annual Report?

3) Are the adjustments consistent from one year to another?

Investors would do best to avoid those companies that issue confusing accounts or those that appear intended to deceive.

Presentation Dissonance

One particular problem to look out for in results presentations and annual reports is when the numbers look bad but the words are full of positive comments – typically about a bright future. Such statements often include comments about the strong financial position of the company, which just means they have not yet run out of cash.

One can call this "presentation dissonance" where an intelligent reading of the numbers would tell a very different story. This undermines confidence that the directors are telling you the truth. Prudent directors do not publish excessively optimistic or bullish comments about future profits or cash flow because the future is always uncertain. Such comments that are made, whether informally or not, are often a sign that the directors are keener to keep the share price up than inform shareholders about the real position of the company.

Director's Comments

Comments by directors about future profits, or how undervalued the share are currently, should be viewed with deep suspicion as responsible directors know better than to make such statements. At best they can refer you to analyst forecasts (i.e. those prepared by a regulated third party).

Another problem that is all too frequent occurs with interim (i.e. half-year) results. The numbers often suggest that analysts' forecasts for the year will not be met, but there are numerous excuses given as to why the second half-year will be better. You should treat them with skepticism.

Conclusion

Clarity of financial and business reporting is a good measure of the quality of the business and its management. A well written, and clear, Annual Report inspires confidence in the company.

Chapter 8 – Investor Checklist

Chapter 8 – Positive Qualities	Tick Here
No emphasis on EBITDA?	
No emphasis on adjusted/underlying profits?	
Few and small exceptional items?	
Accounts easy to understand?	
Accounts prudent and consistent?	
No presentation dissonance?	
Directors comments restrained?	
Well written and clear Annual Report?	

Chapter 9

Systems and Operations

"You build on failure. You use it as a stepping stone. Close the door on the past. You don't try to forget the mistakes, but you don't dwell on it. You don't let it have any of your energy, or any of your time, or any of your space"......... Johnny Cash.

Many businesses fail, or perform badly, because their internal systems and operations are defective. Reliable and effective IT systems are enormously important in the modern world, but there can be just as many problems that arise from poor internal organisation and processes.

Whatever the cause, failures in company operations can be financially damaging and cause them to lose customers in the long term. Damage to the reputation of a company can also mean it fails to attract new customers and can have a direct impact on the share price.

> **Point # 43**
>
> Don't invest in companies with poor systems.

Ideally you need to avoid investing in companies with poor systems.

Some of the Worst Failings

We have already mentioned the Gulf oil disaster that affected **BP** in Chapter 4. This arose from poor safety procedures and inadequate risk assessment.

Banks are another frequent cause of problems because their customers rely on their IT systems to make payments. If customers are locked out of their accounts and cannot access their money, they become disenchanted in only a few minutes.

TSB changed their IT system after the business was separated from Lloyds Bank. In April 2018 all customer accounts were transferred to the new IT software but many customers (as many as 1.9 million) found they were locked out of their accounts or incorrect balances were being reported. This problem lasted for several weeks, resulted in intervention by the regulatory authorities and major damage to the reputation of the business.

Another example was at the **Royal Bank of Scotland** when another software upgrade locked out customers from their accounts in 2012.

Cyber attacks including personal data breaches and simple malicious attacks are another common recent problem. **TalkTalk** had 157,000 accounts including credit card data hacked in 2015 by two teenagers.

All of these failings are symptomatic of poor IT systems and poor management of them. But there are other kinds of operational failings.

In 2017 the shares of **Provident Financial** crashed by 70% after it reorganized its credit collection operations. CEO Malcolm Le May described it as a "poorly executed migration to the new operating model" which resulted in lower collections of money owed by their clients. The company changed from using self-employed agents to employed staff as debt collectors, supported by new IT systems, but the change of business model seemed to be the major issue.

Judging the Quality of Systems and Operations

It's not always easy to judge the quality of company systems as an outside investor, but it's always worth asking about them if you get the chance. For example, when talking to company directors at AGMs or to staff employed by the company. Are they using modern IT systems that are suitable to the current size of the company is one issue at which to look. Do they have lots of "legacy" application systems run on legacy platforms and hardware that are difficult to maintain – very common problems in banks.

Are they planning major system improvements or upgrades in the near future and have they taken appropriate steps to minimize the risks?

One easy question to ask is who is responsible for IT systems in the company and are they at an appropriate level in the organization? Preferably they should be on the main executive committee.

Has the business invested enough in new IT systems and in training staff in the last few years? A problem that can occur is that management choose to minimize expenditure in the short term so as to boost profits without considering the long-term impact.

> **Point # 44**
>
> Has a company maximized short term profit at the expense of improved systems?

It is perhaps not surprising that Fred Goodwin earned the nickname "Fred the Shred" at the Royal Bank of Scotland due to his ruthless cost cutting. Later it emerged that their IT systems suffered from under-investment with experienced staff lost and work "off-shored" or to contractors. Ross McEwan, who took over as CEO, subsequently said: "For decades, RBS failed to invest properly in its systems".

Trade publications, and of course company competitors if you ask them, can often give you some impression of the quality of a business and its internal systems.

Gradual Improvement or Revolution

Gradual improvement of products, services and operations are a common sign of successful businesses. If you look at companies like **McDonalds**, which although it certainly made substantial changes to the way a small burger restaurant could operate in its early years, it was only later that by continual process improvements it managed to dominate its sector of the food market.

It is rare that there are any step changes in the design of products. **Tesla** is perhaps one example of a revolutionary change in automobile design, but the previous 75 years were marked by gradual improvement, i.e. evolution rather than revolution.

The approach to continuous improvement is characterized by the Japanese Kaizen concept that enabled Japanese manufacturers to improve the quality of their products enormously in the years after World War II. From producing low price products that were perceived as low quality, by the 1960s they were building a reputation for very reliable vehicles and other products. One of the beneficiaries of this was **Toyota** that became one of the largest vehicle manufacturers in the world as a result.

> **Point # 45**
>
> Gradual improvement is the key.

A good example of what gradual change can achieve is in the results of **Greggs.** Seen as a rather mature UK bakery products retailer a few years ago, it experienced a renaissance under a new CEO and has moved into more "fast-food" products. More stores have been opened where footfall is high, as opposed to the traditional High Street focus, and the latest product launch is the vegan sausage roll. That has generated large amounts of publicity and sales, but it's a quite trivial product innovation in reality. This was an example of business evolution in essence, as many aspects of the business were unchanged and the production and distribution facilities did not require major changes.

Product revolutions are exceedingly risky. Look at the example of **Rolls-Royce** which in 1971 became bust and had to be nationalized by the Government after delays in development of the revolutionary RB211 aero engine.

So when you look at a company as an investment, do you see a gradual improvement or risky revolutions? But no change is also a danger sign. Greggs was perhaps an example of where past success meant that the business had not changed much for many years while the market had gradually moved away from it. Specialist High Street bakers have mostly disappeared due to the emergence of supermarkets and convenience stores.

It's always useful to visit companies and see their facilities if you want to get an impression of whether they have moved with the times.

One of the most amusing business television programmes in the last few years was the Troubleshooter series in 1990. One of the companies visited by Sir John Harvey-Jones was the **Morgan Motor Company**.

Even from this writer's brief training and career as a production engineer, I could see that their production methods were hopelessly inefficient and old-fashioned. As a family-controlled business, they were producing cars which had not changed much in design either, in much the same way in 1990 as they had done in the 1930s. Although the traditional design was, and is, part of their appeal to car enthusiasts, there was no good reason not to adopt better production methods.

The same principle of gradual improvement rather than "big-bang" changes is one of the foundations of good internal IT systems. The bigger and more complex the project, the more likely it is to fail. Alternatively it runs massively over-budget and over-time. **Abcam** is a good recent example of how an attempt to totally replace a range of "legacy" software systems which had become difficult to maintain has resulted in very high costs at a level that is impacting company profits, and a project that is obviously way behind schedule.

Summary – Change is Good

Change is good in an organization, but too much change can be damaging. Constant reorganization of the management structure and staff responsibilities can demoralize employees. There is a happy medium that is the best scenario. But change in systems and operations should be a constant process to improve product quality and customer service.

Chapter 9 – Investor Checklist

Chapter 9 – Positive Qualities	Tick Here
Good quality systems?	
Dedicated to continuous improvement?	
No risky revolutions in prospect?	

Chapter 10

Financial Analysis

"There are three types of lies -- lies, damn lies, and statistics"..........Benjamin Disraeli

This book commenced in the first Chapter by trying to persuade you that the financial profile of a company does not matter, i.e. that the reported or forecast numbers are of no importance. But it would be remiss of the author to ignore this aspect of investment altogether – otherwise readers might proceed on an investment approach that ignored the numbers totally. That would not be wise.

There are quite a number of books available on the subject that advise you on how to pick stocks based on financial criteria. The book "What Works on Wall Street" by James P. O'Shaugnessy is one of the most thorough at 670 pages, but there are also simpler and shorter books available. That book did show that the commonly considered approach of buying stocks on low price/earnings (P/E) ratios rather than high P/E ratios is a sound investment approach. Such a selection outperformed other stocks over a 45-year period on a retrospective analysis.

Point # 46
Buying stocks on low p/e ratios does work.

Problems with P/E Ratios

It's not all that surprising that such an approach of picking low p/e stocks will work because logically you are simply paying less for a company's earnings. If a company can maintain those earnings, and pay some of them out in dividends, then investors might recognize sooner or later that the shares are cheap and the price of the stock may then rise. So total return will be positive.

But there is great variability in the returns from this investment approach over the years. Such simplistic systems also tend to ignore the risk associated with different shares.

Growth Needs to be Taken into Account

Although investors like using p/e ratios, either historic or forecast, because they are relatively simple to calculate when sometimes investors need to decide in a few seconds whether a share is cheap or expensive, it ignores the impact of the trend in earnings. A company that can grow its earnings, and reinvest those earnings, is potentially much more valuable in the longer term than one whose earnings are static.

Point # 47

Use PEGs to take account of growth in earnings.

A full analysis of the value of future earnings, whether they are growing or declining is best done by doing a Discounted Cash Flow Analysis so as to convert future cash forecasts into a net present value. But few investors use such a technique. Another, simpler way, to adjust for future growth in earnings was proposed by Jim Slater which is the PEG ratio – this is the price earnings ratio divided by the earnings growth rate as an annual percentage over say 3 or 5 years.

Styles Go In and Out of Favour

When the economy is booming, investors like to invest in growth stocks, i.e. ones that are growing earnings at some pace. At the time of writing that tends to mean sectors such as software, technology, internet retailing, biomedical, healthcare, etc. Because of their growth, such companies can be on relatively high p/e ratios - over 20, 30 or even higher. But when boom turns to bust, and the growth vanishes, the share prices collapse.

Small cap stocks have historically been shown to outperform large cap stocks such as those in the FTSE-100 in the long term. But sometimes they go out of favour as investors bid small-cap growth stock prices up to too high a level. When investors become more nervous about the economy or political trends, they suddenly realize the prices are too high when small cap stocks can be risky.

Sectors can likewise go in and out of favour as IT stocks did in the dot.com boom and subsequent bust from which they took years to recover, or the FAANG technology stocks at the time of writing.

Adding More Factors

You can improve investment performance by combining using p/e ratios with other factors such as return on capital, cash flow, dividends paid, gearing, price/sales, price/book value, share price momentum and operating margin. But any formulaic approach that is shown to be effective is also likely to be traded away by other investors fairly rapidly. In other words, there is no magic formula for investment success in the long term.

> **Point # 48**
>
> Using multiple factors can help, but there is no magic formula.

Avoiding Disasters

Before the financial crisis of 2008 many banks improved their returns to investors by gearing up. They managed to pay consistently high dividends to investors by borrowing money to increase their balance sheets, and expand lending to customers. The equity element on their balance sheets remained unchanged. This was in essence risky because when the loans turned out to be questionable or the borrowers started to default (for example in mortgaged backed securities), the capital of banks started to look inadequate and willingness to lend to banks also dropped. Banks started to run out of cash (e.g. at RBS) and equity shareholders were devastated in the resulting financial crisis.

Companies can adopt risky strategies, such as borrowing money and raising gearing, so as to expand operations, do take-overs or launch into new businesses or markets. But that is risky and can be very damaging to investment returns. One good quote on investment from Warren Buffett is "Rule #1: Don't lose money. Rule #2: Don't forget Rule #1". A few shares that you lose money on can devastate the overall return on your investment portfolio. The solution to that problem is partly diversification so you limit the amount you "bet" on any one share.

You could decide that from retrospective analysis of share prices and the financial profile of companies you have produced a perfect formula for predicting which companies will perform well. Even if you take into account the risks associated with a specific company, there is no simple way to measure risk – see Chapter 4 for discussion on that – so a mathematical approach is not easy.

Even if you get the formula right, what worked yesterday may not work today!

Point # 49
Retrospective data analysis can fool you.

I realised the danger of retrospective data analysis when I was a teenager and was forecasting the results of football games based on past data. You could work out a formula to fit the historic results and factors that might affect the results. Such a formula might be a good "fit" to the data and hence was surely useful in forecasting future results. But in reality the correlations were a mirage and the data subject to change. Lengthening the data analysis period was only of limited help.

Numeric analysis and financial ratios are best viewed as a way to assist you in selecting stocks that are likely to be worthy of analysis and may be better bets while avoiding the dogs that have shown they are not good historically at generating profits. In other words, financial ratios can tell you about past performance. As trends tend to persist, that might give you some indications on future performance but in the business world that is far from certain. Good predictive factors tend soon to be traded away.

Stock Screens

There are now many software products and services that will screen stocks based on certain financial criteria. These tend to offer you formulae that are claimed to have been used by master investors or they enable you to construct your own formula. So for example, a Jim Slater screen might be based on the PEG ratio combined with return on capital and share price momentum with a focus on small or mid-cap companies. Such systems often offer multiple screens that you can review a stock against.

But there is one thing very clear from the historic performance of such screens. That is that they may enable you to do better than average over many years, but the performance of individual screens can vary enormously from year to year.

Stock screens should be seen as another useful tool in an investor's kitbag, but as they have no way of taking into account the qualitative factors discussed in this book, they should certainly not be relied on alone. They also assume that you let the selections run for a period of time before redoing the selection, which may not be the best trading strategy.

Some Ratios Don't Work For Some Stocks

One specific problem is that many stock screens are based on the earnings (i.e. profits) of a company. But some companies do not have any profits. They may be too early in their development to be yet generating profits despite rapidly growing sales. Perhaps they are spending large amounts on marketing to expand sales with an eye on future profits, but in the short term that wipes out their current profits. Perhaps they have just hit a temporary problem such as BP with the Macando oil well disaster. In the latter case, one may need to look at underlying profits or take a view on future earnings. But forecasting future earnings is never easy.

Sometimes looking at the price/sales ratio can assist because a company with substantial and growing sales can usually turn them into profits sooner or later – or an acquirer can do so by stripping out the overheads and excessive remuneration.

For companies with substantial fixed assets such as property companies, or plant & equipment, one option is to look at the value of assets relative to the share price – the price/book per share value. That's assuming the assets can be sold at near what is reported as the book value. That's probably true for property companies if there has been a relatively recent valuation of the properties, but for manufacturing companies or retailers it's a doubtful proposition. In the latter cases, a fire sale of the assets may realize only a small proportion of the value.

You only have to look at the accuracy of published analysts forecasts on stocks to understand that they are not much help. Oddly enough they tend to be more accurate on small cap stocks, on which there is less information available, than large cap stocks. There is also the problem that stock prices can be driven by analysts' views rather than the underlying data, particularly in the short term.

Can You Trust Analysts' Forecasts?

Many financial ratios and analysis depend on future forecasts which are mainly published by company brokers. Alternatively they may be published by independent analysts who have been paid for publishing reports on a company. Needless to say, they are not unbiased.

> **Point # 51**
>
> Analysts forecasts are often biased.

Analyst's forecasts tend to be optimistic and there are many more recommendations to buy stocks rather than sell them. It can be better to make your own forecasts so as to overcome such bias.

Financial Analysis and Styles

You can work out all the required financial ratios covered below by yourself, but there are a number of software products or services that save you the tedium of doing it. One which the author uses is Stockopedia which provides a good summary of the key ratios on one screen page, but I use more than one sometimes.

One can get overwhelmed with numbers - what one might call "information overload" in modern parlance. One way to reduce the complexity is to decide on a "style" that you then follow. Common investment styles are "value" and "growth".

Value Investing: Value investing is one of the most widely known stock-picking methods due to the success of Benjamin Graham and Warren Buffett.

The investor tries to find companies where they believe the share price is undervalued by the market. The investor hopes to benefit from the increase in the share price when the market realizes the true worth of the company. In the meantime, the investor may benefit from relatively high dividend payments. The determination of the true value of a company is not however easy.

Investors with a "value" focus tend to select companies on low p/e ratios, high dividends and positive cash flow but with less emphasis on growth. But the danger is that apparently cheap shares can often be cheap for a reason, i.e. they face major strategic or operational issues that are not reflected in the historic numbers.

> **Point # 52**
>
> Apparently cheap shares can be cheap for a reason.

Growth Investing: Growth investing focusses on shares where there is believed to be good prospects for future returns arising from the potential of a company's earnings to grow. The idea is that growth in the company's earnings will drive an increase in the share price. The potential for growth can be driven by factors such as the market on which the company is focused. If it is seen as being in a technology growth sector then earnings should grow even if the management is relatively incompetent. At least that is the theory.

But investors can get over-enthusiastic about companies and sectors as we saw in the dot.com era. They can easily over-pay for growth companies, particularly in bull markets. When everyone is buying shares in a company on the perceived growth "story", and nobody is selling, the share price can quickly reach astronomic levels that are detached from any reality.

> **Point # 53**
>
> Growth investors can easily lose touch with reality.

Wise investors in growth stocks need to keep one foot planted in the value camp to avoid them losing touch with reality. All that really matters is the total return from an investment.

Growth stocks can be inherently risker than value stocks, although some of that risk can be diversified away. With some experience investors are likely to sooner or later develop their own style which is based on your view of relative risk and return. Some investors are clearly more risk averse than others as a facet of their personality while practically the size of their assets, their age and existing financial obligations may affect their chosen style.

What the Author Considers

Having said all the above, I know that readers are likely to be keen for simple advice on financial analysis of stocks. All investors have a preference for simple solutions unfortunately which is why they tend to put too much emphasis on what can be easily calculated.

Below is a list of the numeric factors that the author looks at when considering whether to invest in a stock. Readers who are familiar with financial ratios may wish to skip to the end of this Chapter.

Return on Capital. The return on assets that a company obtains is one of the most important measures of both the competence of management, and the likely long term returns you will obtain from holding a stock.

> **Point # 54**
>
> Return on capital is a measure of management competence.

You can measure return on capital in more than one way, for example as Return on Assets (ROA), as Return on Capital Employed (ROCE) or as Return on Equity (ROE).

Return on Equity ignores the use of debt. The way that a company's debt is taken into account is the main difference between ROE and ROA. In the absence of debt, shareholder equity and the company's total assets will be equal. When debt increases, equity shrinks, and since shareholder equity is the ROE's denominator, its ROE gets a boost. But most trading companies, as opposed to financial institutions or property companies will have moderate leverage and wise investors will not invest in companies with high debt, so in practice the use of one or other formula is not going to make much difference.

So long as you use a consistent formula and a company returns above 15% you can't go far wrong. Just compare that rate of interest with what you will get in a bank deposit account and you will see why it is so good – and there are many companies that achieve more than 15% ROE. The only difference between the two is that company profits are more variable so there is some risk attached to the return.

Such a return means that a company is generating a good return to reinvest in building the business or paying it out in dividends. Usually only a minor proportion is paid out in dividends with the rest being used to finance growth, either organic or by acquisitions. The wonder of compounding does the rest.

The best explanation of why return on capital is so important is probably in Joel Greenblatt's book entitled "The Little Book That Beats the Market". He developed a formula based on return on capital and earnings yield (the inverse of the price earnings ratio) as a stock picking solution. It works well in the long-term but with considerable variation in results over the short term and because it ignores a lot of other factors and quality measures it can be a dangerous system to use just by itself.

This writer certainly considers the return on capital to be one of the most important measures of the quality of a company. It tells you how efficiently the management are using the capital entrusted to them. But return on capital can be distorted by past write-offs of assets and the use of leases as opposed to the purchase of capital assets so you need to be wary of those points.

> **Point # 55**
>
> Return on capital is a one of the most important measures of the quality of a company.

Price/Earnings Ratio and PEG. The price earnings ratio is a simple measure of how much you are paying for the earnings of the company. As covered earlier in this Chapter, the PEG ratio aims to allow for the benefit of growth in earnings.

The P/E Ratio is generally considered to indicate a cheap share if it is less than 15. Another way to look at this is to consider the inverse ratio which is the earnings yield. A P/E of 15 equates to an earnings yield of 6.7% which is again of course a lot better than the interest you would get on a bank deposit account at the time of writing, and as earnings are likely to grow when deposit interest does not, it's even better than you might think at first glance. You can just add the growth percentage to the earnings yield percentage to give you the likely total return.

Cash Flow. Good companies generate positive cash flows, i.e. they end up with more cash at the end of the year than at the start. That's ignoring acquisitions and financing activity. Cash generated from operations before tax (operating profit after adjusting for non-cash items) is

> **Point # 56**
>
> Profits need to turn into cash.

always clearly stated on the "Cash Flow Statement" in accounting reports. It should preferably exceed the Operating Profit. If it does not it means the profits are not turning into cash. This may happen because under accrual accounting, revenue and profits may be recognized but the cash may come in much later than the normal accounts receivable payment terms. Measures of Free Cash Flow per share are often used by investors as an alternative to earnings per share figures, because cash can be considered of more importance.

Margins. The difference between what a company is selling its products or services for, compared to its directly related costs, is the Gross Margin. The figure after all overhead administration costs is the Net Margin. Clearly the higher these numbers are the better.

> **Point # 57**
>
> Margins vary a great deal between industry sectors.

But the margin numbers vary a great deal between different industries. Supermarkets for example, have very low margins – typically below 3% which they offset by having very high volumes of sales to produce decent overall profits in relation to capital.

Other companies such as those based on strong IP, or intangible assets or where they are dominant market players can have very high margins. For example, property portal **Rightmove** has a Net Margin (operating profit divided by revenue and expressed as a percentage) of 60% at the time of writing. In other words, the majority of the sales revenue turns into profit. But that is quite unusual!

It's best to compare a company's margins to other companies in the same sector to see whether they are exceptional or not. Companies with very small margins are vulnerable to profits disappearing when the economy or their sector is in difficulties – they can even run out of cash and go bust in such circumstances. Very high margins tend to eroded away by competitors entering the market unless a company has some monopoly power or barriers to entry.

Price/Sales Ratio. The price/sales ratio (alternatively called the revenue multiple) indicates how much you are paying for the revenue of a company and can be a useful measure when there are no reported profits or when you are comparing companies in the same sector. But it is very much sector dependent. Retailers, particularly super-

> **Point # 58**
>
> Use price/sales ratio when there are no profits.

markets, tend to have high revenue but low margins and often poor cash flow. Just because such companies have enormous amounts of revenue that potentially could be turned into profits does not, in practice, mean that they manage to do so.

In early stage technology companies, price/sales may be a useful indicator if the revenue is growing and profits are in sight. It can be a good measure of what a trade buyer may pay for a company, after stripping out the overheads. A multiple of 2 times is conservative and can be as high as 10 times or more where the technology is seen as being particularly exciting.

Share Price Momentum. One commonly followed investment strategy is to buy shares that are going up and sell those that are falling. Or in your own portfolio, buy more of the winners and sell the losers.

Momentum can be a very successful investment approach, up to a limit, because there is a clear short-term correlation in share prices. Those shares that rise in price today are likely to rise tomorrow.

However there are also dangers with this strategy as it can lead to wild market swings as investors jump onto hot stocks and dump those out of favour. As James Goldsmith said: "If you see a bandwagon, it's too late".

Dividends. Private shareholders typically like dividends because it means cash in their pockets that they can spend. Those in retirement are particularly enamoured of dividends to support their lifestyle. But this is a false view. What matters is the total return – the capital appreciation in the share price plus dividends. You can always turn capital appreciation into cash by selling a few shares and that might also be more tax efficient. However, dividends are a good indicator of two things.

> **Point # 59**
>
> What matters is total return, not dividends paid.

Firstly it tells you the company is actually generating enough surplus cash to pay it out in dividends. Secondly it reflects the confidence of the directors in the future as they tend to avoid reducing annual dividends. It may also indicate that the directors cannot find a useful project in which to invest the cash, i.e. they have run out of opportunities or ideas – that's a negative sign.

A company would typically expect to pay out a third of its earnings in dividends, with the rest reinvested in the business. But high growth early stage companies may choose to reinvest all of the earnings and not pay a dividend. That is not unwise if the opportunities are there. Companies where the **Dividend Yield** is higher than 5% or where the **Dividend Cover** (the amount of the earnings divided by the dividends) is low should be looked on with suspicion. Those companies that are financing dividends by borrowing money are particularly dubious. Companies can use any surplus cash to either pay dividends or repay debt and in many cases it is clearly preferable to do the latter, but companies are reluctant to reduce dividends or remove them.

The advantage of dividends is that they cannot be taken away from investors, once paid. It also gives the investor the choice as to whether to invest them again in the same company's operations, or invest in other assets. It avoids the risk of the management wasting the reinvested cash on loss-making projects or acquisitions. A bird in the hand is worth two in the bush is a saying to remember.

Debt, Gearing and Interest Cover. Companies may finance their activities through either equity or debt. Debt may be cheaper, or more expensive, depending on various factors such as the current level of interest rates, but high debt adds risk. The lenders will require onerous covenants and if profits decline the company may end up in the hands of the bankers.

Investors in a company's equity shares should avoid those with high or unsustainable debts. Two simple measures of that are the Gearing which measures the proportion of debt to equity in the business, and the Interest Cover. The latter tells you how many times the interest that is being paid is covered by a company's earnings. Five or more times is preferable.

Current Ratio and Altman Z-Score. Companies only go bust when they run out of cash and cannot pay their creditors. That's clearly something shareholders should avoid. A good measure of the ability of a company to meet its short-term obligations is the Current Ratio, the current assets (cash plus stock typically) divided by the current liabilities (typically trade creditors and short-term debt). A ratio of higher than 1.4 is preferable for trading companies, but there are exceptions.

> **Point # 60**
>
> Companies only go bust when they run out of cash.

Software companies where customers have paid in advance for maintenance or support may have low current ratios because those advance payments are treated as short-term liabilities when in reality they will never be "repaid". Retailers are often at the other extreme because they have the habit of paying their suppliers after they have sold the purchased stock to customers who pay cash.

A more sophisticated measure of credit risk is the Altman Z-Score which takes into account a few more parameters. A score below 1.8 is a negative indicator.

Asset Values. Traditionally companies used to be valued on their assets, with assets per share being the measure used. If the share price is less than the **Assets Per Share**, or book value per share as it is otherwise known, then in theory the company could sell its assets, wind up and return the surplus to shareholders. Or someone else, typically known as an "asset-stripper", could bid for the company and do the same. But in the modern world most company shares are priced at a multiple of assets because shareholders are more interested in their earnings capacity.

> **Point # 61**
>
> Assets per share are now rarely a useful measure.

The assets are relatively undervalued partly because they may not be effectively valued by conventional accounting, e.g. the company's profits may depend on brands, IP or customer relationships rather than fixed assets such as property, plant and machinery. Property companies, and to a lesser extent building companies, are exceptions though where investors do look at the assets per share. Even if assets are fairly valued, they often include a lot of intangible capitalized software development or goodwill. Those may not be realizable if the company falls on hard times.

Sales or Profits Per Employee. In service companies where revenue is often dependent on workforce activity levels, another useful measure is revenue per employee. It can be particularly useful for comparing companies in the same sector as a measure of how effectively they are utilising their staff. Profits per employee also tell you whether the company is charging good rates for their work or not. UK companies report their number of employees in their Annual Report.

R&D Spend. The level of Research & Development expenditure as a proportion of revenue, or per employee, can be a useful measure of how much a company is investing in the future.

Again, it's useful to compare it to the level of other companies in the same sector. Hopefully R&D spend will turn into future profits, but it does not always.

Assets That Are Difficult to Value

Here's a useful quotation from Richard Beddard writing for Sharescope on why **Fundsmith** has been one of the best performing funds in recent years: "Fundsmith seeks to invest in businesses with intangible assets, brand names, market dominance, patents, large installed bases to service, distribution networks that give them more reach than their competitors, and deep relations with clients. It is often nigh on impossible to value these assets, so accountants rarely bother".

Trends More Important

As said before, financial accounts tell you about the past, not about the future, while analysts' forecasts of future numbers are generally unreliable. But the trends in the numbers may tell you something about the future.

Extrapolating existing trends in the revenue, margins and profits is a good way to predict the future numbers. But sometimes a step change is forecast. This may arise because of an acquisition or disposal, new Government regulations, a change of management, or simply a more optimistic view of the company's prospects. Such changes need to be closely scrutinized – they are often optimistic forecasts.

For example, many acquisitions are not as successful as hoped. The buyers tend to pay too much, when the sellers know when it is a good time to exit. Remember also this Warren Buffett quotation: "When a management with a reputation for brilliance tackles a business with a reputation for bad economics, it is the reputation of the business that remains intact".

Chapter 10 – Investor Checklist

Chapter 10 – Positive Qualities	Tick Here
Is there growth in revenue and profits?	
Is growth fairly valued?	
Is Return on Capital high?	
Are the P/E and PEG Ratios not too high?	
Do profits turn into cash?	
Are the margins adequate?	
Are other financial ratios OK?	
Company qualifies under stock screens?	
Is the share price momentum positive?	
Are dividends paid, but not too high?	
Is the debt low and interest cover high?	
No at risk of running out of cash?	
Not at risk of major business changes?	

Chapter 11

Trusts and Funds

"I think those who invest in mutual funds want someone else to do the thinking for them".....Ron Chernow

Many private investors hold a mix of direct share investments and funds. The latter can provide exposure to sectors that the investor knows little about such as companies operating and listed in foreign countries. This Chapter covers some of the aspects of investing in funds that are different and which have not been covered in previous chapters.

There are primarily two kinds of funds – open ended ones such as Unit Trusts and OEICs, and closed ended ones such as Investment Trusts. The former have the advantage of trading near their net asset values and have to buy or sell portfolio shares based on investor demand for their fund – this can be positively dangerous if the fund holdings are illiquid such as in direct property holdings, or some are in small cap or unlisted companies as we saw in the **Woodford Equity Income** debacle. Such problems can cause a fund to temporarily close to redemptions.

Closed end investment trusts are listed investment companies whose shares trade in the market in the normal way. They can trade at a discount, or premium, to the value of their underlying holdings. Investment trusts have conventional Annual General Meetings where you can meet the investment manager and where investors can have a say in the activities of the company. Investment trusts can hire and fire their fund manager. Investment trusts often have lower costs and can also borrow money to enhance their returns. As a result they often return better performance than equivalent open ended funds. For those reasons this writer tends to prefer investment trusts to other kinds of funds.

Consistent Long-Term Performance

A key measure of the merit of a fund is its long-term performance against similar funds or its benchmark. For investment trusts this information is readily available from the AIC.

Active Versus Passive

Funds can be active or passive. Passive funds are those which simply choose to follow an index, i.e. they are index trackers where no decisions are made as to the merit of individual holdings. Shares are bought or sold simply on the trends in the chosen index constituents. Such funds should be lower cost than active funds as the fund managers do not need to research companies or monitor them.

There is a healthy debate about the relative merits of active versus passive funds. Depending on market conditions, and the skill of active managers, active funds can do better or worse than the market. But the performance of active funds depends on the stock picking skills of the fund manager when few can demonstrate consistent and persistent outperformance.

An Experienced Fund Manager With A Process?

For active funds, the experience of the fund manager and their historic performance is usually a good indicator of their likely future performance. But not always so – fund managers can lose their touch or become over confident in their own abilities, as appeared to happen with the previously lauded Neil Woodford.

One issue to examine is whether a fund manager has a consistent and effective process for selecting investments if they are an active manager. It is important that they are not simply making ad-hoc decisions about investments however experienced they are. Such a process is often documented in the Annual Report of an investment trust, or is covered in presentations at the AGM.

Point # 62

Does the manager have a process?

The risk of a fund manager, or their fund management company, losing their touch, means it is wise not to name a fund or trust after the fund management company or individual.

Not A Closet Index Tracker

One kind of fund to avoid are those that claim to be active managers but in reality have holdings that closely follow their benchmark index. These are called "closet" index trackers. Such funds tend to charge the higher fees that are associated with active management but will never outperform their benchmark.

Low Cost

One of the key aspects to look at for funds is their overall costs – both management and other costs. As John Bogle has pointed out in his books, funds with lower costs consistently give higher returns to investors. In other words, the argument you have to pay more to get the best fund manager does not hold water.

> **Point # 63**
>
> Investors should always favour lower cost funds.

Not Too Large

The larger a fund grows, the more its performance tends to approximate to its benchmark. But funds that are small can be illiquid.

Board Engaged and Independent

A key aspect to look at in investment trusts is how closely the board of directors monitors the activity of the fund manager, and how independent they actually are from the manager. As investment trusts solely have non-executive directors, they are often dependent on the fund manager. This can be a particular problem in Venture Capital Trusts which are often created by a fund manager and who line up the initial directors. They also advise on subsequent director appointments and directors often serve on more than one company run by the same fund manager.

Where there are long-serving directors in investment trusts they often appear to develop a rather close relationship with the fund manager which can prejudice their decisions about whether to change fund manager or on revisions to fees.

Investment trusts often have directors who have served more than nine years which is contrary to the UK Corporate Governance Code as they are no longer considered "independent" if they serve for longer than nine years. Such companies should be avoided by investors as the directors can become stale and ignore important trends in the markets.

Performance Fees

There is no evidence that performance fees in funds actually improve the investment performance of the fund manager. In reality they tend to simply add to the costs imposed on investors. But performance fees are beloved by fund managers and they often persuade the directors of investment trusts to implement them. However some performance fee arrangements are worse than others. Those that pay out in the good times, but don't reduce future payouts in bad times are particularly to be avoided.

Point # 64

Investors should avoid funds with performance fees, or those that are too complex.

Performance fees can sometimes be so complicated that even the directors of investment companies and their fund managers do not understand what the result will be. But you can be assured that when interpretation is doubtful, the payout will err on the side of the fund manager. You should avoid investing in funds where the performance fee is incomprehensible.

Controlled Discounts

Investment trusts can trade at substantial discounts to their net asset values, particularly in bear markets or where the shares are relatively illiquid.

Good investment trusts usually have some discount control mechanism in place to manage the discount such as a share buy-back mechanism, regular tender offers or wind-up provisions.

Reasonable Discount

Discounts or share price premiums that are high can indicate that an investment company is deeply unpopular with investors, or excessively popular. The latter can cause the share price to collapse if the market perception of the company suddenly changes.

High discounts can appear to be bargains as it suggests that you can buy the underlying assets at a discount to their market value by buying them via an investment trust. But it can also mean that the trust has a record of picking dud investments. High premiums or high discounts are to be avoided.

Look at Underlying Holdings and Their Performance

To judge whether a fund manager is competent it helps to look at the underlying companies in which they invest. Are they investing in companies that show a high return on capital while being on relatively low P/Es and with significant growth in earnings or are they investing in shares that appear to be simply cheap? Are they picking

Point # 65

Is the fund manager picking quality shares?

companies that are of high quality – in other words displaying the characteristics covered in the first few chapters of this book?

AGMs – Are They Well Run?

Good investment trusts have well attended Annual General Meetings with an informative presentation from the fund manager. Few open-ended funds have meetings for investors but Fundsmith Equity Fund is one commendable exception.

How the Chairman handles the meeting, and their willingness to answer extended questions can also provide an indication of their competence.

Informative Annual Reports

The Annual Report of an investment trust can reveal a great deal about the directors and the fund managers. It should clearly explain the main impacts on fund performance in the past year and highlight any particularly disappointing investments (even if they have been subsequently sold) or particular winners.

Chapter 11 – Investor Checklist

Chapter 11 – Positive Qualities	Tick Here
Consistent long-term performance?	
An experienced fund manager?	
Not a closet index tracker?	
Low cost fees?	
Fund not too large?	
Board engaged and independent?	
No performance fees?	
Controlled discount to NAV?	
Reasonable discount?	
Good underlying holdings?	
AGMs well run?	
Informative Annual Report?	

Chapter 12

Key Lessons & Conclusion

"An investment in knowledge pays the best interest"........Benjamin Franklin

To recap on the key message in this book: you need to look at many other factors than the financial ratios of the company to determine whether it is a well-managed business that will repay your investment in the long term. Other parameters than the historic financial ratios are likely to be more important.

Research, Research, Research

There is one clear certainty in the investment world. Those investors who do well do a lot of research. They tend to start with a good education on business and financial matters, and have learned more from experience. When they are looking to invest in the shares of a company, they learn as much as possible about it and do not just look at the financial ratios.

They may read what others have to say about a company, but they do their own research to confirm that the views of others are accurate.

But it's a mistake to think that you can select a stock to purchase, and then forget about it. Indeed it is very unwise to plunge into a large holding in a company until you have held it for some time. The longer you hold the shares in a company, the more you learn about it.

Clearly you should make sure you read all the RNS announcements that a company issues, but you should also monitor the general and financial press for commentary on a company. You should also attend any Annual General Meetings of the company – you'll be surprised at what you can learn there – and at other meetings where management do a presentation.

You could also monitor bulletin boards and blogs for comments on companies but that is usually not a productive exercise because they are so full of ill-informed comments that you have to wade through them to find the rare nuggets of useful information. In other words, it's not a good use of your time.

Note that researching or monitoring companies that operate or are listed in overseas countries can be particularly difficult. Some countries are better than others in relation to providing financial information on companies – the USA is particularly good, but even so you may have difficulty in tracking companies there unless you are familiar with the market. In other countries, language can provide a barrier to learning all you need.

The time spent on company research and on monitoring a company has to be limited to some extent. There's a cost/benefit ratio here to be taken into account. Experience can tell you which are the best sources of information.

Learn From Your Mistakes

One thing the author does is to keep a record of the financial profile of a company, and what prompted me to invest in it, when I make the first investment in the shares. I keep that document forever. Some day I will go back and do some analysis of that data over the last 25 years. But in the meantime, I do review every share trade and holding at the end of each calendar year to see where I lost or made money during the year.

One useful aspect to look at is whether the share trades you made actually contributed to your overall portfolio performance, or detracted from it. If you have kept a record of your portfolio holdings at the end of each year, it's easy to carry those forward with the latest prices to the end of the next year.

Private investors should at least attempt to work out their portfolio performance on an annual basis. If they cannot beat the stock market indices then you would be best to let someone else manage your assets. But few private investors do such calculations or have software that gives them the answer.

Conclusion

I hope this book has provided some useful information and food for thought about the investment process. The author would welcome any comment on the content or suggestions for improvement. He can be contacted via the Roliscon web site here: https://www.roliscon.com/contact.html

Chapter 12 – Investor Checklist

Chapter 12 – Positive Qualities	Tick Here
Have you done enough research?	
Can you easily monitor the company?	

Investor Checklist Summary

Chapter 2 – Business Models and Competitive Strategy	Tick Here
High barriers to entry?	
Economies of scale?	
Differentiated product/service?	
Low capital required?	
Hard switching costs?	
Proprietary technology and IP?	
Smaller transactions?	
Repeat business?	
Short term contracts?	
Diverse clients?	
Diverse suppliers?	
Network effect benefits?	
Regulations creating barriers to entry?	
Business model simple & understood?	
Competitive threats understood?	
Established market?	
Sector I like?	

Chapter 3 – Market Position, Branding and Marketing	Tick Here
Multiple products/services?	
Strong brands and trade marks?	
Leading market positions?	
In harmony with economic trends?	
Clear value propositions?	
Competent marketing?	

Chapter 4 – Controlling Risk	Tick Here
No major business risks obvious?	
No new competitors apparent?	
Low risk of technological obsolescence?	
Markets not subject to change?	
No risk of Government regulation?	
No risk of product development failure?	
Little risk of process failure?	
Low risk of reputation/brand damage?	
Management judged competent?	
Low risk of fraud/false accounting?	
Low debt?	
Low exposure to exchange rate risk?	
Few business acquisitions?	
No foreign adventures?	
Are the management risk averse?	

Chapter 5 – Rational Pricing and Good Margins	Tick Here
Prices rationally set?	
High margins?	

Chapter 6 – Company Culture, Structure & Pay	Tick Here
Appropriate culture?	
Founders no longer running the business?	
Independent chairman?	
Appropriate corporate structure?	
Motivated and happy staff?	
Rate highly on ESG measures?	
Reasonable remuneration for directors?	
Not too generous with perks?	

Chapter 7 – Company Regulation and Governance	Tick Here
UK or US domicile?	
Subject to UK Takeover Panel Code?	
Adhere to corporate governance code?	
Large director stakes, but not too large?	
All directors have big shareholdings?	
Not too many directors?	
Directors do not have too many roles?	
Past prejudicial share placings?	
AGMs at convenient time & place?	
AGMs well run?	
Past prejudicial share placings?	
Share buy-backs being used?	
Liquid shares with low bid/offer spread?	
Too much speculative interest?	
No big legal disputes?	
No big pension liabilities?	
You have read the Annual Report?	
Directors can be trusted?	

Chapter 8 – Presentation of Accounts	Tick Here
No emphasis on EBITDA?	
No emphasis on adjusted profits?	
Few and small exceptional items?	
Accounts easy to understand?	
Accounts prudent and consistent?	
No presentation dissonance?	
Directors comments restrained?	
Well written and clear Annual Report?	

Chapter 9 – Systems and Operations	Tick Here
Good quality systems?	
Dedicated to continuous improvement?	
No risky revolutions in prospect?	

Chapter 10 – Financial Analysis	Tick Here
Is there growth in revenue and profits?	
Is growth fairly valued?	
Is Return on Capital high?	
Are the P/E and PEG Ratios not too high?	
Do profits turn into cash?	
Are the margins adequate?	
Are other financial ratios OK?	
Company qualifies under stock screens?	
Is the share price momentum positive?	
Are dividends paid, but not too high?	
Is the debt low and interest cover high?	
No at risk of running out of cash?	
Not at risk of major business changes?	

Chapter 11 – Trusts and Funds	Tick Here
Consistent long-term performance?	
An experienced fund manager?	
Not a closet index tracker?	
Low cost fees?	
Fund not too large?	
Board engaged and independent?	
No performance fees?	
Controlled & reasonable discount to NAV?	
Good underlying holdings?	
AGMs well run?	
Informative Annual Report?	

Chapter 12 – Key Lessons	Tick Here
Have you done enough research?	
Can you easily monitor the company?	

Index

A

4Imprint, 81
Abcam, 89
Accelio, 8
Access to distribution channels, 20
Access to limited resources, 20
Accounts may mislead, 15
Accrual accounting, 12
Acquisitions, 49
Active versus passive, 108
Adjusted cash, 79
Adjusted EPS, 79
Adjusted profits, 78
Adjusted revenue, 79
Administration, 47
Advertising, 40
Agency problem, 75
AGMs, 71, 111
Agricultural product producers, 36
AIC, 108
AIM, 66, 68
Airlines, 32
Alcoholic drinks, 43
Alternative measures, 17
Altman Z-Score, 48, 103, 104
Amazon, 15
America Online, 49
Amey, 11
Amortization, 77
Andy Grove, 41
Annual General Meetings, 71, 111, 113
Annual Report, 74
Anthony Pulbrook, 46
Apple, 25, 35
Articles of a Company, 66
Asset Values, 104
Assets, 13
Assets per share, 104
Asset-stripper, 104
Audit committee, 67
Autonomy, 11, 47, 49
Axioma, 60

B

Banks, 30, 44, 47, 81, 85
Barriers to entry, 20, 22, 42
Bass, 36
Benjamin Disraeli, 91
Benjamin Franklin, 113
Benjamin Graham, 96
Berkshire Hathaway, 24, 42, 59
Beta, 41
Beware the Zombies, 8, 53
Bhopal, 45
Bid/ask spread, 73
Bid/offer spread, 73
Bill Hewlett, 56
Blogs, 114
Book value per share, 104
Boots the Chemists, 24
Boston Consulting Group, 60
Box-ticking, 68
BP, 41, 85, 95
Bradford & Bingley, 44
Brand recognition, 40
Brand valuations, 38
Branded products, 36
Branding, 35
Brewers, 36
BT Plc, 74
Building companies, 104
Bulletin boards, 74, 114
Business acquisition risk, 48
Business model, 14, 19, 26
Buy-backs, 72

C

Capita, 11
Capital requirements, 20, 24
Capitalization of software
    development costs, 78, 104
Car manufacturers, 21, 36
Carillion, 11
Cash flow, 100
Cattles, 11
Cedar Group, 11
CFD providing, 31
CFDs, 44
Channel Islands, 65

Chevrolet Corvair, 45
Chinese AIM companies, 46, 65
Chris Boxall, 81
Clinical trials, 44
Closed ended, 107
Closet index tracker, 109
Clothing retailers, 32
Coal companies, 61
Coca-Cola, 36, 43
Commodities, 36
Companies Act, 46, 66
Company cars, 64
Company Structure, 58
Competence of management, 14, 46
Competing on price, 22
Competition, 21
Competitive Strategy, 19
Comply or explain, 58
Confusing accounts, 82
Conglomerates, 59
Connaught, 11
Consignia, 38
Construction companies, 23, 32
Consultancy firms, 33
Controlled discounts, 110
Controlling risk, 41, 51
Controlling stake, 69
Conviviality, 11
Copyright laws, 22
Corporate Governance Code, 66
Corporate sponsorship, 64
Costa Coffee, 59
Covenants, 103
Credit card data, 45
Culture, 55
Current ratio, 48, 103
Cyber attacks, 86

D

Dave Packard, 56
David Cummings, 55
Debt, 103
Debt for equity swaps, 47
Debt Risk, 47
Deepwater Horizon, 41
Defined benefit schemes, 74
Defined contribution schemes, 74
Delcam, 63
Depreciation, 77

Diageo, 36, 38
Dick Fuld, 58
Dictators, 58
Differentiated products, 22
Director share sales and purchases, 70
Director's comments, 83
Discount control mechanism, 111
Discounted cash flow, 12, 15
Discounted placings, 72
Discounts, 111
Discounts to net asset values, 110
Diverse clients and suppliers, 23
Dividend cover, 102
Dividend yield, 13, 102
Dividends, 102
Domicile, 65
Dominant personality, 56
Drug development companies, 29

E

Earnings yield, 100
EBITDA, 13, 77
Economies of Scale, 20
Electronic hardware producers or distributors, 32
Elon Musk, 56
Enron, 11
Entertaining clients, 64
Entrepreneur, 56
Entrepreneurial companies, 58
Environmental damage, 61
Environmental, Social and Governance, 60
Erinaceous, 11
ESG, 60
Ethically dubious businesses, 61
Ethically Sound, 61
Exceptional items, 78
Excess profits, 42
Exchange rate risk, 48
Executive Chairmen, 58, 68
Exploration companies, 30
Exporters, 48
Extortion case, 45
Extraordinary items, 78, 79

F

FAANG, 93
Facebook, 15, 25, 37, 38, 56
FairFX, 79
False accounting, 47
Fashion retailers, 32
FCA, 44, 66
Fevertree, 25
Financial analysis, 91
Financial Conduct Authority, 66
Financial crisis in 2008, 30, 62
Financial products/services, 43
Financial ratios, 10
Financial regulation, 26
Financial Reporting Council, 66, 79
Findel, 11
Flash offices, 64
Ford Motor Company, 24, 35, 56
Ford Pinto, 45
Foreign adventures risk, 49
Forward exchange contracts, 48
Founders, 56
FRC, 66
Fred Goodwin, 14, 57, 64, 87
Free cash flow per share, 100
Fresh & Easy, 49
Funds, 107
Fundsmith, 28, 105
Fundsmith Equity Fund, 111

G

Gambling companies, 61
Gearing, 48,103
George Bernard Shaw, 50
Gin distillers, 36
GlaxoSmithKline, 80
Globo, 11, 46, 47
Gold mining companies, 29,36
Good to Great, 57
Goodwill, 104
Governance, 65
Government subsidies or
    regulations, 20
Greggs, 88
Gross margin, 100
Growth investing, 97
GSK, 80
Gulf oil disaster, 85

H

Harvard Business Review, 53
HBOS, 11, 31
Health food companies, 32
Healthcare Locums, 11
Henry Ford, 56
Hewlett-Packard, 56
Hierarchical structures, 59
High pay, 62
How to Run a General Meeting of a
    Public Company, 71
HP, 47, 49
HSBC, 82
Humble personalities, 57

I

IFRS, 12, 13
Importers, 48
Incentive schemes, 62
Index trackers, 108
Information overload, 96
Insolvency, 47
Insurance and other financial
    companies, 31
Intangible assets, 38, 101
Intel, 37, 41
Intellectual property, 20, 22
Interest cover, 48, 103
Interest rates, 103
Iinternet gaming companies, 31, 61
Investment companies, 68
Investment managers, 33
Investment trusts, 68, 73, 107
Investors Champion, 81
Investors in People, 60
IP, 101
i-Phones, 35
Isle of Man, 65
iSoft, 11
IT security, 45

J

Jack Cohen, 56
James Goldsmith, 102
James P. O'Shaughnessy, 91
JetForm, 8

Jim Collins, 57
Jim Slater, 15, 92, 94
Joel Greenblatt, 99
John Bogle, 109
John D. Rockefeller, 65
John Maynard Keynes, 11, 17
Johnny Cash, 85
Joint ventures, 59
Just Eat, 79

K

Kaizen, 88

L

Land grab, 16
Large or small director share stakes,
   69
Law and Practice of Joint Stock
   Companies, 46
Lawson, Roger, 8
Leading brand positions, 37
Leapfrogging by competitors, 32
Learning advantage, 20
Legal disputes, 74
Lehman, 58
Ling-Temco-Vought, 59
Liquidity, 73
Listing Rules, 46, 66
Lloyds Banking Group (LLOY), 30
Lloyds of London insurance market,
   31
Long term contracts, 23
Long-Term Incentive Plans, 62
Lord MacLaurin, 57
Low calorie diet products, 43
LSE, 66
LTIPs, 62
LTV Corporation, 59
Luke Johnson, 58, 70

M

Mam, M., 53
Management, 14
Margins, 53, 100
Mark Zuckerberg, 56
Market position, 35

Market purchases, 72
Marketing, 35
Marmite, 36
Mature companies, 59
Maximizing prices and revenue, 53
Maxwell Communications, 11
McDonalds, 87
Medical products, 43
Michael Porter, 19
Microsoft, 21, 22
Mining companies, 29, 36
Mitie, 11
Modern portfolio theory, 41
Monopolies, 25, 26
Monopoly or oligopoly, 44
Morally dubious businesses, 31
Morgan Motor Company, 89

N

Natural monopolies, 25
Natural resource companies, 30
NCC Group, 11
Neil Woodford, 108
Net margin, 100, 101
Network effects, 20, 25
Newspaper industry, 51
Nomination committee, 67
Non-executive directors, 67, 68, 70
Normalized EPS, 79
Northern Rock, 11, 44

O

OEICs, 107
Oil/gas companies, 29, 61
One product companies, 35
Only the Paranoid Survive, 41, 51
Open ended, 107
Open offer, 72
Operating margins, 54
Overboarding, 70

P

P/E Ratio, 13, 91, 100
Patents, 22
Patisserie, 11, 46, 47, 58, 70
Pay, 55

Payday loan companies, 61
PEG ratio, 15, 92, 99
Pension liabilities, 74
Pepsi, 43
Performance fees, 110
Perks, 64
Personal information, 45
Peter Drucker, 35
Petrofac, 64
Pharmaceutical products, 44
Plus500, 44
Polly Peck, 11, 47
Prejudices, 28
Premier Inns, 59
Presentation dissonance, 83
Presentation of accounts, 77
Price Earnings Growth, 15
Price optimization, 53
Price sensitive information, 66
Price/book per share value, 95
Price/Earnings Ratio, 13, 99
Price/Sales Ratio, 95, 101
Pricing, 53
Pricing power, 36
Private jets, 64
Proactive Systems, 8
Product competently marketed, 39
Product differentiation, 20, 21
Product marketing, 39
Product or service differentiation, 22
Product risks, 12, 17
Production process risk, 44
Profits, 13
Profits per employee, 104
Prohibition, 43
Property companies, 13, 48, 104
Proprietary products, 22
Proprietary technology, 20
Prospectus, 42, 46
Provident Financial, 86
Puffing, 73
Purplebricks, 16

Q

QCA, 69
Quindell, 11, 47
Quoted Companies Alliance, 69

R

R&D spend, 104
Rational pricing, 53
Recruitment companies, 33
Registered trade mark, 36
Regulation, 65
Regulations, 26
Regulatory News Announcement, 66
Regulatory risks, 61
Remuneration, 62
Remuneration committee, 67
Remuneration Guidelines, 63
Research & Development expenditure, 104
Retailers, 23, 101, 103
Retailing, 50
Return on Assets, 98
Return on capital, 22, 25, 54, 98
Return on Capital Employed, 98
Return on Equity, 98
Revenue multiple, 101
Revenue per employee, 104
Richard Beddard, 105
Rightmove, 101
Rights issue, 71
Risk adjusted returns, 17
Risk of failure to develop a new product, 44
Risk of fraud and false accounting, 46
Risk of government regulation, 43
Risk of management incompetence, 45
Risk of market changes, 43
Risk of new competitors, 42
Risk of reputation and brand damage, 45
Risk of technological obsolescence, 43
Risk takers, 51
Risky behaviour, 62
RNS announcements, 66, 70, 72, 113
ROA, 98
ROCE, 98
ROE, 98
Roger Lawson, 8
Roliscon Ltd, 2

Rolls-Royce, 37, 80, 81, 88
Ron Chernow, 107
Rosiello, R., 53
Ross McEwan, 87
Royal Bank of Scotland, 11 , 14, 45,
    57, 86, 87
Royal Mail, 38

S

SAAS, 23
Safe Port Act, 61
Safestore, 60
Sarah Gordan, 58
Sector that you like, 28
Segmenting markets, 22
Seveso, 45
Share buy-backs, 72
Share placings, 71
Share price momentum, 101
Share price premiums, 111
Share rampers, 73
Sharescope, 105
ShareSoc, 63, 71
Shorters, 73
Short-term speculators, 73
Silverdell, 11
Sir John Harvey-Jones, 89
Small cap stocks, 92
Small transactions or large, 22
Soap producers, 36
Social media, 45
Socialist governments, 44
Soft drinks, 43
Software as a service, 23
Software companies, 22, 23, 103
Speculation, 41
Speculative interest, 73
Spread-betting, 31
Steel companies, 24, 32
Step change, 105
Stock screens, 10, 94
Stockopedia, 96
StreamServe, 8
Structure, 55
Styles, 96
Succession, 56
Superior return on capital, 42
Supermarkets, 54, 100, 101
Switching costs, 20

SWOT analysis, 18
Systems and operations, 85

T

Takeover Panel Code, 65
TalkTalk, 86
Technology companies, 48, 101
Tender offers, 72, 111
Terry Smith, 28, 31
Tesco, 49, 54, 56, 57
Tesla, 21, 56, 87
The Little Book That Beats the
    Market, 99
The Signs Were There, 47
Third-party suppliers, 25
Tim Steer, 47
Time Warner, 49
Tip sheets, 74
tobacco companies, 61
Too many directors, 70
Too many jobs, 70
Torex Retail, 11
Total return, 102
Toyota, 88
Trade mark, 36
Trade Mark Registration, 37
Traded companies, 68
Trends, 105
Trusts, 107
TSB, 86
Tylenol, 45

U

UIGEA, 61
UK Corporate Governance Code, 58,
    110
UK Individual Shareholders Society,
    63
Underlying profits, 13
Unilever, 36
Unit trusts, 107
Unlawful Internet Gambling
    Enforcement Act, 61
Unlisted, 68
Unprofitable companies, 16
Utilitywise, 11

V

Value Investing, 96
VCTs, 73
Venture capital trusts, 73, 109
Vertical integration, 24
Victor Bennett, 55
Volatility in a share price, 41
Volume of share trades, 74

W

Warren Buffett, 19, 20, 24, 28, 30,
  42, 53, 77, 93, 96, 105
Web site, 40
What Works on Wall Street, 91
Whitbread, 59
White-collar Crime in Modern
  England, 46
Willie Sutton, 47
Wind-up provisions, 111
Woodford Equity Income, 107
Worldcom, 11